UNIVERSITY POLITICS

This entertaining new account of Cambridge around the turn of the twentieth century contains the complete text of F. M. Cornford's famous satire of 1908 on University politics, *Microcosmographia Academica*, together with a full account of the controversies which gave rise to it.

Cambridge during this period was being subjected to pressure for reform from within and outside the University, forcing it to change the content of the existing syllabuses and to extend the range of subjects taught; to alter the balance between teaching and research, and the relationship between the Colleges and the University; to develop modern science in the curriculum; to widen University membership, above all by admitting women; to question the influence of religion; and to raise funds without compromising the University's independence to do what it liked. All these matters, many of which remain in debate at the end of the twentieth century in Cambridge and in the wider academic community, provoked fierce debates and provided a rich context for Cornford's pamphlet. The book contains a selection of contemporary photographs and portraits, some not previously published.

Francis MacDonald Cornford, LittD, FBA (1874–1943), by Eric Gill. Cornford came up to Trinity College in 1893, was elected to a Fellowship in 1899 and became Laurence Professor of Ancient Philosophy in 1931. The drawing dates from 1929.

UNIVERSITY POLITICS

*F. M. Cornford's Cambridge and his advice
to the young academic politician*

GORDON JOHNSON

CAMBRIDGE
UNIVERSITY PRESS

Published by the Press Syndicate of the University of Cambridge
The Pitt Building, Trumpington Street, Cambridge CB2 1RP
40 West 20th Street, New York, NY 10011–4211, USA
10 Stamford Road, Oakleigh, Melbourne 3166, Australia

© Cambridge University Press 1994

First published 1994
Reprinted 1995, 1996, 1998

Printed in the United Kingdom at the University Press, Cambridge

A catalogue record for this book is available from the British Library

Library of Congress cataloguing in publication data

Cornford, Francis Macdonald, 1874–1943.
[Microcosmographia academica]
University politics: F. M. Cornford's Cambridge and his advice to the young academic politician /
[edited by] Gordon Johnson.
p.   cm.
ISBN 0 521 46919 8 (pb)
1. University of Cambridge – History – 19th century – Humor.
2. University of Cambridge – Administration – History – 19th century – Humor.
I. Johnson, Gordon, Ph. D.   II. Title.
LF119.C67   1994
378.42'65–dc20   93–46115   CIP

ISBN 0 521 47547 3 hardback
ISBN 0 521 46919 8 paperback

FOR
FAITH JOHNSON

Contents

Illustrations

Introduction

On 27 February 1908, the editors of the *Cambridge Review* announced that they had 'received from Messrs Bowes and Bowes one of the most amusing little pieces of Cambridge satire published in the last decade. For the modest sum of one shilling net, the young academic politician may obtain a *Microcosmographia Academica*, in which the various parties in University politics are hit off more nearly to the truth than they will like.'[1] Indeed, the picture painted in *Microcosmographia Academica* of the political life of an exceptionally intelligent and well-informed community, dedicated to the pursuit of knowledge and the quest for truth, was far from flattering. In University politics, so it appeared, matters were not settled by genuine discussion, with participants ready to modify their opinions in the light of the argument of others, or as a result of new information becoming available during the course of a debate. Instead, the scholar was characterised as being deeply conservative, sceptical and mocking in his attitude towards reform, and, in all his political actions, conditioned by greed and fear. So charmingly, however, was this unpalatable message conveyed, that *Microcosmographia Academica* has acquired a lasting fame, at least in the limited social world of Oxford and Cambridge high tables; and occasionally learned references are made to it in the columns of the broadsheets and the literary reviews. Its crisp formulations of the Principle of the Wedge, the Principle of the Dangerous Precedent or the Principle of Unripe Time (which are, in effect, not real arguments but rhetorical devices designed to make dialogue impossible) are glibly bandied about by many who lack a true understanding of either the original text or its purpose.[2] The author of the anonymous pamphlet was Francis MacDonald Cornford, then a young Fellow of Trinity College,

---

[1] *The Cambridge Review: A Journal of University Life and Thought* (hereafter, *CR*), 27 February 1908, 262.

[2] *Microcosmographia Academica* is now usually quoted without irony by ultra-conservatives in support of reaction. See, for example, the remarks made by A. Williams in the Discussion in the Senate on 13 July 1993, *Cambridge University Reporter* (hereafter *Reporter*) 1992–3, 1022.

a former editor of the *Cambridge Review*, and later to be the first Laurence Professor of Ancient Philosophy in the University.[3]

ৡ

Francis Cornford was born on 27 February 1874 at Eastbourne, the second son of the Revd James Cornford and his wife Mary Emma MacDonald. He was educated at St Paul's School and went from there to Trinity College, Cambridge, where, among a distinguished group of students taught by a formidable group of dons, he became a favourite pupil of Henry Jackson. Cornford distinguished himself by being in the first division of the first class in parts I and II of the Classical Tripos in 1895 and 1897, and was bracketed equal with A. E. Bernays, his contemporary at Trinity, for the Chancellor's Classical Medal. Two years after graduating he became a Fellow of Trinity and was appointed to the teaching staff in 1902. In 1909 he married Frances Darwin, the poet and daughter of Sir Francis Darwin, whom he had met as a pupil of Jane Harrison at Newnham. Apart from service during the war of 1914–18, first as a sergeant-major and musketry instructor at Grantham (he had been an excellent shot at Bisley), and then in the Ministry of Munitions, his whole life was dedicated to the pursuit of classical scholarship at Trinity and Cambridge.

As a classicist, Cornford became impatient with what he held to be a dry and exhausted scholarly tradition. At first he was much guided by his Trinity mentors Henry Jackson and A. W. Verrall. The latter in particular was imparting in his lectures a way of interpreting the great classics of ancient literature as one would a work of modern poetry or prose: 'not reading back our own ideas into the ancient mind – far from it – but boldly applying common sense and universal critical canons to the content of a work, and daring to teach that the thought of an author was more important than his syntax'.[4] But soon after his election to a Fellowship, Cornford came much under the influence of Gilbert Murray, whose translations of Euripides were appearing at that time, and of Jane Harrison, whose *Prolegomena to the Study of Greek Religion* was published in 1903. Jane Harrison was a brilliant teacher. Cornford recalled that for her and for her audience a lecture was a dramatic event: 'Once she enlisted two friends to swing bull-roarers at the back of the darkened lecture-room in order that the audience might learn from the "awe-inspiring and truly religious" sound what Aeschylus meant by "bull-voices roaring from somewhere out of the

---

[3] Biographical information about Cornford from: *Times*, 5 January 1943, 6; D. S. Robertson, 'Francis MacDonald Cornford', *CR*, 30 January 1943, 164–5; Gilbert Murray, 'Francis MacDonald Cornford 1874–1943', *Proceedings of the British Academy 1943*, 421–32; Reginald Hackforth, 'Cornford, Francis MacDonald', The *Dictionary of National Biography* (hereafter *DNB*) *1941–1950*, 177–9; W. K. C. Guthrie, 'Memoir', in F. M. Cornford, *The Unwritten Philosophy and other Essays*, ed. W. K. C. Guthrie (Cambridge, 1950), vii–xix.

[4] Guthrie, 'Memoir', xii–xiii.

1   Jane Ellen Harrison (1850–1928), Fellow of Newnham College and
classical scholar. This portrait was painted by Augustus John in the summer of
1909 and given to Newnham College by Miss Harrison's friends.

unseen".'[5] Murray, while being a little critical of Miss Harrison's 'lack of early training
in the drudgery of exact scholarship' and her 'natural impulsiveness', recognised her
'width of learning, a force of historical imagination, and an infectious interest in her
subject which amounted to genius'.[6] Her great contribution was to point to the
importance to any understanding of Greek religion of a study of actual ceremonies and

[5] F. M. Cornford, 'Harrison, Jane Ellen (1850–1928)', *DNB 1922–1930*, 408. Among Miss Harrison's student
friends at Newnham were Mary Paley (who married Alfred Marshall), Margaret Merrifield (who became Mrs A. W.
Verrall) and Ellen Crofts (who married Francis Darwin), *ibid*.
[6] Murray, 'Cornford', 421.

rites rather than just a concern with the fictional and largely artificial figures of the Olympian gods. Cornford was encouraged to approach ancient texts afresh by trying to devise ways of uncovering the often unstated inherited concepts and beliefs and methods of thinking which lay behind them. His first book, *Thucydides Mythistoricus*, published in 1907, sought to explain how a highly scientific and logical mind, like that of Thucydides, expressed itself in a language which did not yet possess a scientific or logical vocabulary. Leonard Woolf, reading it in his exile in the Colonial Service in Ceylon, wrote to Lytton Strachey that he thought it to be 'rather good, except that as a book it has the almost universal fault of not ending.'[7] Others found it stimulating but flawed; though none could deny that Cornford's 'idea was a fruitful one, and the singular beauty of the writing made the book memorable'.[8]

In his later years, Professor Guthrie tells us, Cornford 'said that it sometimes seemed to him as if he had been all his life writing one and the same book'.[9] A dominant concern runs through all his work. In his inaugural lecture in 1931, he expressed it thus: 'If we look beneath the surface of philosophical discussion, we find that its course is largely governed by assumptions that are seldom, or never, mentioned. I mean that groundwork of current conceptions shared by all the men of any given culture and never mentioned because it is taken for granted as obvious.'[10] Cornford was attempting the exposition of what he perceived as a basic truth about the nature of human thought, and then applying that truth in particular to the Greeks. His key studies *From Religion to Philosophy* (1912) and *The Origin of Attic Comedy* (1914) broke new ground in this way in the understanding of ancient religion and philosophy. In Murray's words, Cornford

> with his 'sound scholarship' and his calm philosophic insight . . . obtained a constant and vivid awareness of the world of assumptions and ways of thought which lies under the surface of ancient philosophy and poetry, and indeed of ancient language itself; but he used that awareness of the undercurrents as an instrument for the fuller understanding of the upper streams. To understand Heraclitus or Anaximander, to understand even Plato and Aristotle, it was necessary to realize the atmosphere of thought and feeling in which they lived, and the habits of thought which they had accepted by inheritance and without criticism from primitive ages.[11]

The classical scholar had also to remind himself that many words had no straightforward English equivalent, and also that those that did carried with them different meanings and implications in different times: *words move . . . only in time; words strain, crack and sometimes break, under the burden, under the tension, slip, slide, perish, decay with imprecision, will not stay in place, will not stay still.*

---

[7] Woolf to Strachey, 15 September 1907, in Frederic Spotts (ed.), *Letters of Leonard Woolf* (London, 1989), 132.
[8] Murray, 'Cornford', 423.
[9] Guthrie, 'Memoir', viii. [10] Quoted *ibid.*, viii. [11] Murray, 'Cornford', 425.

Cornford's mature work dealt with Plato's most difficult thought and came to fruition with a series beginning in 1935 with *Plato's Theory of Knowledge*. 'These later books', wrote Donald Robertson, one of Cornford's own pupils at Trinity, 'show a deep maturity of power and judgment, without losing the arresting quality of his earlier writing'.[12] But in wrestling with Plato, Cornford seems to have shied away from applying fully to a study of the ancient Greek texts the insights of contemporary philosophy. As Geoffrey Lloyd has written, it is somewhat intriguing that Cornford's works are

> far less influenced by the philosophy being done at Cambridge at the period when they were written than one might have expected. It is not that they are philosophically naive: they exhibit a far subtler reading of Plato than that judgement would suggest and though they now show their years they are still read, and still worth reading, which is more than can be said for most Plato scholarship of the 30s. But it's surprising how little FMC seems to have got out of contemporary philosophy – and that despite the fact that many of the most exciting developments were the work of FMC's own colleagues at Trinity.[13]

Along the way, Cornford had also devoted much time to work with the dying Philip Wicksteed on a translation, with introduction and commentary, of Aristotle's *Physics*, which was published in the Loeb Library in 1929 and 1934. And after the series of books on Plato, he returned, in 'Principium Sapientiae', which was published after his death in the collection of essays edited by Guthrie, to one of his central original interests: the relationship between philosophy and its pre-philosophical background. Although it appears that Cornford was a little defensive about some of his own early work, it is clear that he continued to be very interested in the problems of the relation between religion and philosophy, and Hocart, Hooke and others provided him with his opening to try a new approach.[14] Guthrie characterised the qualities he found in all Cornford's writing: 'the living (not mechanical) symmetry of form, the grace and delicacy of the details, the humour, irony and occasional fantasy enlivening a fundamentally serious theme'.[15]

Besides his own writing, Cornford was the original moving force behind 'Cambridge Classical Studies' which did, and does, so much to promote the publication of new classical scholarship. Although a quiet man – he could be 'embarrassingly silent', and Virginia Woolf was quite intimidated by him[16] – Cornford had a reputation as an eloquent and exciting lecturer. He was deeply committed to bringing his scholarship to a wider public, and a course of four lectures for the University's extra-mural

---

[12] Robertson, 'Cornford', 165.   [13] G. E. R. Lloyd to G. Johnson, 10 May 1993.   [14] *Ibid.*
[15] Guthrie, 'Memoir', xix.
[16] Robertson, 'Cornford', 165; And 'he looks like something carved in green marble on a tomb. This has the effect of making him very silent.' Virginia Woolf to Ottoline Morrell, 16 August 1911. Nigel Nicolson (ed.), *The Flight of the Mind: The Letters of Virginia Woolf 1888–1912* (London, 1975), 474–5. Also, 'Too much elderly brilliance for my taste.' Virginia Woolf to Vanessa Bell, 12 August 1908, *ibid.*, 351.

programme resulted in the publication in 1932 of *Before and After Socrates*. 'A student in any branch of knowledge', he wrote in the preface to the book,

> who is invited to set before a popular audience, within the space of four hours, the gist and upshot of his studies, may do well to submit himself to the discipline implied. He knows that the expert will frown upon some of his statements as questionable in content and dogmatic in tone, and will mark the omission of many things for which no room could be found. But it will do him good to sit back in his chair and look for the main outline, so often obscured by detail.[17]

Along with G. M. Trevelyan he was a great friend of the Working Men's College in London, and he took infinite trouble, with his pupils, to entertain visitors from the College when they came to Cambridge. Shortly before his death, he completed a translation of Plato's *Republic* – 'a masterpiece of vivid rendering, which reads like a new book.'[18]

Cornford died in Cambridge on 3 January 1943. Those who mourned him pointed to his love of music, taking up the viola in his fifties in the hope that eventually he might rustle up a full family orchestra, and of poetry, especially that of Milton and the seventeenth century. They also wrote of his personal charm and of

> the essential beauty of his character, the gentleness, the unselfishness, the utter remoteness from all that is worldly or violent . . . His relations with a series of brilliant children, whose opinions were at times vehemently opposed to his own, and whom he encouraged to 'sail away like ships' in pursuit of their own ideals, were a model to those parents who believe in the supreme power of affection and the value of freedom.[19]

Robertson testified to the deep impression Cornford had made on him as a shy freshman at Trinity forty years earlier. 'That charm never faded, and his death is a personal loss of which it is impossible to write.'[20]

Cornford's *Microcosmographia Academica*, which he included in its proper chronological place in his list of publications in *Who's Who*, is an elegant satire on University affairs at the turn of the nineteenth and twentieth centuries, exhibiting some of the qualities to be found in his academic work: light in tone, and deftly written, there is a fundamental seriousness about it and its argument is profound. It belongs to a tradition of humorous literature, much then in vogue, and one which, in the University, found an outlet in the *Cambridge Review*. This journal, founded in 1879, was published

[17] F. M. Cornford, *Before and After Socrates* (Cambridge, 1932; reprinted 1960), ix.
[18] Robertson, 'Cornford', 165.
[19] Murray, 'Cornford', 432.   [20] Robertson, 'Cornford', 165.

weekly during Term, designed neither to amuse nor to edify the University but to be 'a part of it'. As one of its originators wrote later:

> It did not require much wit to see that a society of the importance of the University of Cambridge needed a journal in which its life and thought should be reflected; and the experience of a generation has now shewn that there is room for such a journal so long as it defines the University in the broadest sense, and does not affect to despise either the research of the learned or the athleticism of the muscular.[21]

By design its editorial team consisted of an undergraduate, a BA and a senior member of the University. Around the turn of the century, besides acting as a weekly news-sheet, the *Review* carried vigorous and opinionated pieces of prose and light verse on University affairs. Many were frivolous or satirical in tone. Cornford himself contributed a number of poems over his initials, and some of the unsigned paragraphs appearing from 1900 bear an uncanny resemblance to the argument and style of *Microcosmographia Academica*. Late Victorian and early Edwardian Cambridge was a fruitful subject for such satire because it seemed that only reluctantly and with obvious difficulty were the University and the Colleges transforming themselves into places of learning and research appropriate for the times. Feeling at once radical and conservative, religious and secular, reforming and reactionary, poor and rich, independent and oppressed, the dons might be forgiven for not seeming to know where they were going, and for appearing to make such a foolish display of managing their affairs.

What distinguishes *Microcosmographia Academica* from other early twentieth-century light literature, however, is that Cornford's tract contains a remarkably clear-eyed general analysis of political organisation and the use of power. Beneath the elegant and witty prose lies a profound (if somewhat pessimistic) argument about human political behaviour: reason plays but small a part in politics, for people are driven more usually by prejudice and fear.[22] Those who wish to get things done must understand how human nature is and how it might be worked upon. They must be cynical and ruthless in their methods, and recognise the unattractiveness of the world in which they tread. Cornford may not have been a skilled political practitioner, and, while recognising how necessity drives the political world, he must surely have regarded politics with distaste; for like Machiavelli's advice to his Prince, Cornford's essay bears the marks of a guileless and open-hearted man recollecting in a mood of resignation how that which

---

[21] *CR*, 21 February 1907, 261. The *Review* became a financial success, however, reaching a regular circulation of around 1,600, because its proprietors decided to carry in full the text of the weekly University sermon – essential reading in parsonages throughout the country; and later they published as a supplement a termly list of members of the University in residence.

[22] In April 1972, Dr G. S. R. Kitson Clark, a Fellow of Trinity, inscribed a copy of *Microcosmographia Academica* which he gave to Dr Kenneth Easton. At that time Dr Easton was battling with officials and committees in the National Health Service over the establishment of a sensible scheme of emergency care for patients after accidents. Dr Kitson Clark wrote: 'nowadays it is necessary to remember that people can be bolted in two directions. The dominant motive is still fear, but men can not only be frightened from doing right they can be frightened into doing what is judicious.'

needs and should be done is checked, thwarted and threatened, by fear, by the inadequacies of others, and by the play of the political system. The disciplined exercise of pure reason transformed frustration with the petty politics of College and University into as perfect a piece of satire as may be imagined. Although the direct experience upon which Cornford drew was that of Cambridge in the early 1900s, it reflected an ancient and universal human condition. Venturing forth from Trinity at the outbreak of the Great War, Cornford found that when it came to politicians 'the academic species is only one member of a genus wider than I had supposed'. Others vouched for the general applicability of Cornford's analysis, noting that 'Civil servants and businessmen alike have claimed to recognise in their own walks of life the types which it portrays.'[23] Cornford's beautifully written, ironic and funny but so true a commentary on human political activity thus outlives its occasion and its generation.

Cornford published a second edition in 1922, revealing his authorship and dedicating the work to his friend Edward Granville Browne, the great scholar of Persian literature and Sir Thomas Adams's Professor of Arabic, who, in the face of establishment hostility and indifference, sought to explain to the West the new spirit of nationalism which was sweeping Persia, and to impress upon his colleagues in Cambridge the importance of studying and teaching the living languages of the Middle East.[24] *Microcosmographia Academica* was reprinted in 1933, and then, after Cornford's death, Professor Guthrie wrote a new preface to an edition published in 1949, and it has been reprinted several times since then. Cornford himself resisted the temptation to revise or expand his text, recognising the difficulty of recapturing 'the mood of the fortnight in which this book was written'. But after nearly ninety years he may have sympathised with the desire of one from another age to probe below the surface of his text to find what lies beneath it. Cambridge at the turn of the century was a different world; but it is a familiar one also. Some account of the situation in which *Microcosmographia Academica* was written not only allows us to understand detail which the passage of time has rendered obscure, but it helps a fuller understanding of the essential and universal truth of the text itself. And, as Cornford was heard to say after a lecture attempting a similar exercise on the Pre-Socratics, I have found him and his times *'inexhaustibly* interesting'.[25]

---

[23] Cornford, preface to the second edition of *Microcosmographia Academica*; Guthrie, 'Memoir', 425.
[24] E. D. Ross, 'Browne, Edward Granville (1862–1926)', *DNB 1922–1930*, 123–5; Sir Peter Swinnerton-Dyer has also helped me on this point.
[25] Quoted by Murray, 'Cornford', 425.

Cornford's Cambridge

Between the mid-nineteenth century and the outbreak of the Great War, Cambridge was transformed from a rather indifferent academy into a great University. In part this was the result of demands from outside the University, but to a large degree it was also a consequence of enthusiasm for change from within. The politicians who clamoured for Royal Commissions and Parliamentary visitations to break down the social and religious exclusiveness of the ancient Universities, who wanted them to teach useful subjects, and to promote research in science and technology, found a willing response from within the academic community. But during these years, scholars whose vocation was contemplative, reclusive and quiet were being asked to do more, and to change more quickly, than many of them had ever imagined had happened to dons before. The change was neither easy nor comfortable, nor was it a foregone conclusion that Cambridge (and the other long-established seats of learning) would meet the challenge posed by the rapidly changing society and economy of nineteenth-century Britain. Many of those who saw a need to compete, adapt and push forward were often concerned that reform would be thwarted and opportunities would be lost. As E.V. Arnold, a founder of the *Cambridge Review*, observed in February 1907, 'no criticism of the University is harder for its devoted *alumni* to answer than that which maintains that here, more than anywhere else in the world, a decorous self-repression is reckoned a higher quality than either activity or enterprise'.[1] But move Cambridge did; and we should not be surprised if, in coming to terms with a new order of things, the University did not sometimes appear as ridiculous as it was brave.

ૐ

[1] *CR*, 21 February 1907, 261.

9

2   His Grace the Duke of Devonshire, Chancellor, 1892–1908, leads the honorary degree procession round the Senate-House Yard, 11 June 1892, following luncheon in the large gallery at the Fitzwilliam Museum. Among the fifteen honorary graduands were HRH the Duke of Edinburgh, the Viscount Cranbrook, the Earl of Northbrook, Joseph Chamberlain, John Morley, Professor Seeley and Leslie Stephen. A Guard of Honour of 100 rank and file from the 4th (Cambridge University Volunteers) Battalion, Suffolk Regiment, was drawn up on the lawn and received the procession with a royal salute.

It has always been difficult to describe the University of Cambridge and how it works, for it is one of those peculiar forms of social organisation which have evolved for the express purpose of creating, discovering, preserving and transmitting knowledge. In order to function effectively, a University requires that dedicated scholars, teachers and students come together in one place where they are able to enjoy the use of relatively secure material resources, free from undue interference from those who do not share immediate membership of their society with them. Although it is part of a larger world, the University is also essentially a world of its own, conceiving of itself as a whole contrasted with other wholes in society at large. In formal terms this finds expression in the fact that the University of Cambridge is a corporation which, in addition to the usual characteristics of such bodies, like owning property, possesses the power of conferring degrees, of exercising disciplinary authority over its members and, in the period with which we are now concerned, of returning two representatives to Parliament.

At the turn of the century, it was reckoned that there were about 13,000 or 14,000 members of the University of Cambridge. Of these, about 3,000 were undergraduates, most of whom (but by no means all, because it was far from unknown in those days for students to interrupt their period of study by time away from Cambridge) were in residence with the intention of taking a degree. Nor was the undergraduate body the academic elite which it was to become later in the twentieth century. Although in this, as in almost every aspect of University life, major change was taking place, it was still the case in the early 1900s that a fifth of the undergraduates did not actually complete degrees, a third still aimed for an ordinary BA degree, study for which could be spread over many years, leaving just under half studying for an honours degree, which normally had to be completed in a minimum of nine consecutive terms of study.[2] The University's educational role so far as its students were concerned was thus conceived as being quite broad: to produce the well-rounded citizen rather than to focus too narrowly on the training of the mind. It could easily accommodate the likes of Sammy Woods who resided 'as a member of his college for 12 terms, playing rugger and cricket for Cambridge, while failing monotonously to pass the university entrance exam'.[3]

Academic qualifications for admission consisted of tests in mathematics, Latin and Greek. These were not particularly stringent and the necessary standards could have been obtained at many good schools in the country. (Ironically, as admissions criteria became tougher it may have been that, initially at least, the range of schools from which students came to Cambridge narrowed somewhat.) A candidate needed to satisfy a tutor in one of the Colleges that his attainments were sufficient to enable him 'to pass the University examinations in due course'; have a certificate of good moral character, usually from his headmaster; provide information about his birth and parentage; and reveal 'the name and address of the parent or guardian responsible for

---

[2] Based on figures compiled by J. A. Venn for 1902–6, *CR*, 30 January 1908, 193, 196.
[3] Noel Annan, 'Singing the Blues', *London Review of Books*, 15 April 1993, 15.

3   The heart of the University, *c.* 1900. To the left of the Senate-House is the
University Library; across the street on the extreme right, the west end of Great
St Mary's, the University Church. Dominating the area is part of Gonville and
Caius College, rebuilt to designs by Arthur Waterhouse in 1870. At this corner,
as Professor Pevsner notes with disapproval, 'the building blossoms out into a
tall tower with *tourelles*, a spire, big chimneystacks, a monumental gateway
below, and statuary in niches, in fact everything the architect could think of'. A
powerful reminder that for much of Cambridge's history the University has
co-existed in complex and sometimes difficult relationships with Colleges.

the payment of the College accounts'.[4] Competition to gain admission was not particularly stiff. Indeed, young men were advised that anyone who was able to comply
with the conditions listed above

4   *The Student's Handbook to the University and Colleges of Cambridge: Second Edition Revised to June 30, 1903* (Cambridge,
     1903) (hereafter *Handbook*), 18–19.

has little difficulty in obtaining admission to a College at short notice, but it is important for those who wish to have rooms in College to apply for admission a long time beforehand; and if an applicant has any special preference – either for expensive rooms, or cheap rooms, or for rooms in a particular situation – it is in general desirable that he should begin his correspondence with the College at which he wishes to enter, at least twelve months before the commencement of residence.[5]

It was usual, but not essential, to come up to Cambridge to begin a course of residence and study in October, at the start of the academical year.

Further education at Cambridge was, of course, relatively expensive. Detailed specimen budgets were drawn up as a guide for prospective students from 1902 onwards. These showed that, depending on the proposed course of study, preferred College and personal habits, an undergraduate would need anything between £40 and £75 to cover settling-in costs and then an income of somewhere between £107 5s 0d and £225 10s 0d thereafter to meet recurrent annual expenditure. In other words an undergraduate needed to find, on average, about £160 (roughly £7,850 at today's prices) a year to study in Cambridge.[6] At a time when a good professorial stipend was about £500 a year, and when many large families made do with less than a tenth of that, it is clear that cost alone limited the number of those coming to Cambridge. While it is true that there were large numbers of scholarships and prizes available for the very able, few of these alone would have done more than meet a third, or perhaps half, of the sum needed to see an undergraduate through his course; and it was one of the recurring criticisms of the older Universities generally that their endowments failed to meet their original purpose of providing for the education for the really poor scholar.

Once in residence, the young well-heeled undergraduate found himself in a community which, while opening up the prospect of a relatively free and easy social life, was hedged by peculiar tribal rules enforced by fierce fines and petty punishments. The legal age of majority was still twenty-one, and tutors stood to their pupils *in loco parentis*. Undergraduates were expected to attend chapel services, at least on Sundays, unless they had been given permission not to do so. All sorts of attempts were made to keep the undergraduates from the clutches of immoral women, horses and gambling; and shopkeepers in the town who extended credit too generously were put out of bounds to the students. The Proctors and their men patrolled the streets and, picking up men for misdemeanour or riot, could have them confined to their rooms in College, fined multiples of 6s 8d or even expelled.[7] Smoking was prohibited when wearing a gown, or under any circumstances in the courts of the Colleges (though in this latter

[5] *Ibid.*, 19.   [6] *Ibid.*, 55–78.   [7] *Ibid.*, 49–54.

regard Cambridge was out of step with her sister Oxford).[8] Students were required to wear 'their proper Academical Dress at all University Lectures and Examinations, . . . in the University Church, the Senate-House and the Library; in the streets at all times on Sundays, and on other days after dusk'.[9] The requirement that gowns be worn in the town during daylight hours on Sundays was not repealed until 1921,[10] and undergraduates had to wait until the heady days of 1965 before they were legally free to roam the streets at night attired like other citizens.[11] The main activity of the Proctors seems to have been to prevent street fighting, which they did with only varying success, and to raise revenue from the gownless youth, at which they were quite adept.

Provided that certain prescribed formalities were fulfilled, and all proper dues paid, a man could remain a member of the University for the rest of his life. Most graduates were 'engaged in the ordinary work of the world – the army, navy, civil service, the church, the legal and medical professions, or commercial pursuits of various kinds',[12] and the most important right attaching to membership of the University was that to share in the government of the University itself. The ultimate decision on all questions of academic policy rested with the Senate: a body which included, roughly speaking, all those men, whether they continued to live in Cambridge or not, who had taken a Bachelor's degree and had subsequently, on payment of a further fee, become a Master of Arts or Master of Laws.[13] *The Student's Handbook to the University and Colleges of Cambridge*, first published in the Michaelmas term of 1902 by the University Press, has in its second edition the clearest and most concise description of the rights of these senior graduates:

> The Senate has full power by means of Graces[14] to legislate for the University, provided that it does not infringe the University statutes, which rest on the higher authority of the King in Council, and ultimately upon an Act of Parliament. It is the Senate also that allows degrees, appoints most of the University officers, and elects the two members who represent the University in the House of Commons.[15]

[8] 'In all that concerns the graces of life we are supposed to be behind our Oxford friends, but in two or three points we claim to cut a better figure. We consult appearances by not smoking in College courts as they do. No doubt Oxford and Cambridge both smoke too much, but over-indulgence in the Indian weed is no modern vice, if a general one. James I, we believe, sent a letter here to prohibit its use at St Mary's Church! We can hardly imagine a grave ecclesiastic preaching "athwart the smoke of burning weeds," as Tennyson has it.' *CR*, 26 November 1896, 106.

[9] In this formulation, the regulation goes back to that proposed by the Council of the Senate in their *Report* of 19 June 1882 (*Reporter 1881–2*, 740, 747; *cf. Ordinances of the University of Cambridge to 1 October 1908* (hereafter *Ordinances 1908*) (Cambridge, 1908), 303).

[10] *Reporter 1920–1*, 986, 1108.

[11] *Reporter 1964–5*, 1031–2, 1203–6, 1266, 1815, 1817–19. Students who were Bachelors of Arts (or of BA status) were exempted from wearing gowns in the streets after dark in 1961.

[12] *Handbook*, 1.

[13] They had also to remain on the books of their Colleges, which might also involve the payment of a small annual fee.

[14] Grace: in this sense originally a dispensation, granted by the Congregation of a University, or by some Faculty in it, from some of the statutable conditions required for a degree, leading in Cambridge to mean any decree of the Governing Body – i.e. of the Senate (*Oxford English Dictionary*).

[15] *Handbook*, 2.

4   The University and its influential friends: His Grace the Duke of Devonshire, Chancellor, with members of the royal family and honorary graduands, on the steps of the Hall of King's College, following the degree ceremony, 27 June 1894. HRH the Duke of York (later King George V) was among those receiving an honorary degree. Left to right: Dr Sandys (the Orator), HRH the Princess Victoria, HRH the Duke of York, HRH the Princess Maud, HRH the Princess of Wales, the Earl Cathcart, Mr Alexander Peckover (the Lord Lieutenant of Cambridgeshire), the Chancellor, Mr Pell, Sir John Thorold, Sir R. N. F. Kingscote, the Duke of Richmond and Gordon, HRH the Prince of Wales (later King Edward VII), Mr Ernest Clarke.

Such a large, dispersed and heterogeneous body, however, could not be expected to administer the University. Executive authority rested in theory with the Chancellor; but by custom the Chancellor was a dignitary not usually resident in Cambridge (between 1861 and 1908 this office was held successively by the seventh and eighth Dukes of Devonshire, both of whom significantly influenced University affairs from afar), and authority devolved in practice upon his deputy, the Vice-Chancellor, who was appointed annually from among the Heads of Colleges. Again, by custom not breached between 1719 and 1991, the person appointed Vice-Chancellor served for no more than two consecutive academical years at a time.[16] Associated with the Vice-Chancellor was the Council of the Senate, which was elected under certain restrictions by those whose names appeared on an Electoral Roll – mainly the 600 or so MAs who were resident in Cambridge. Besides its executive functions, the Council had an important position in regard to legislation, as no Grace could be put to the Senate unless it had first received the sanction of the Council.

Other officials and groups of persons discharged special executive functions within the University, but the permanent administrative staff was really very minimal. The most important officials were the two Proctors, elected annually by the Senate from persons nominated by the colleges in turn, who were responsible for University discipline; the Registrary, who kept the archives and received the fees payable for degrees (from 1891 to 1910 this office was held by John Willis Clark who combined responsibility for managing the University with a prodigious output of books and learned articles); and the Librarian (from 1889 to 1921, Francis John Henry Jenkinson, whose portrait by John Singer Sargent is one of the finest in Cambridge) who had custody of the books of the University.

The Senate also appointed Syndicates[17] and these were of two sorts: those which were of a permanent nature to administer various departments of University business, such as the Library Syndicate, the Press Syndicate, the Botanic Garden Syndicate or the Local Examinations Syndicate; and those which were established for some special

[16] Thomas Gooch (Gonville and Caius) was elected Vice-Chancellor in 1717, 1718 and 1719; Sir David Williams (Wolfson) in 1989, 1990 and 1991. Others served for more than two years in all, but not consecutively – e.g. Henry Cookson (Peterhouse) in 1848, 1863 and 1864, and John Power (Pembroke) in 1870, 1871 and 1878. In 1989, the Syndicate appointed to consider the Government of the University (commonly known as the Wass Syndicate, after its chairman, Sir Douglas Wass) recommended that 'the Vice-Chancellor be a full-time office and that the holder be required to give up any other College or University office' (*Reporter 1988–9*, 641). On 1 October 1992, Sir David Williams, who had resigned as President of Wolfson College, became the first Vice-Chancellor since John Copcot in 1586 to hold the office without also being a Head of House. The Regent House also agreed, following a ballot on a recommendation in the Wass Syndicate's Report, that the Vice-Chancellor should hold office for five years, renew-able for two (*ibid.*, 1990–2, 285), but the Council, noting that 'By the end of the current academical year Sir David will have held office . . . for three years . . . have agreed to recommend that he be appointed [to the new style office] for four years from 1 October 1992' (*ibid.*, 1991–2, 130). The recommendation was approved, Grace 1 of 22 January 1992 (*ibid.*, 335).

[17] Syndicate: a council or body of Syndics – a Syndic in Cambridge being a term applied to members of special committees of the Senate, appointed by Grace for specific duties (*Oxford English Dictionary*).

purpose, like the Syndicates responsible for overseeing the construction of particular buildings, or that set up 'to consider the mode of election to Livings in the gift of the University with reference to the provisions of clause 7 of the Benefices Act of 1898',[18] which were discharged when their particular task was done. In addition, there were Special Boards of studies deputed to superintend University teaching and examinations in the various subjects of study, but unless they were contemplating changes in the curriculum, or nominating examiners for appointment by the Senate, they had nothing like the work later associated with the Faculty Boards which grew out of them. Each department of study was under the control of a Professor, and in those subjects where the College interest was weak – for example in nearly all the sciences save mathematics – the health of the department depended upon the Professor. Where research, rather than undergraduate teaching, was seen as the main academic interest (again in most of the sciences) it was the Professor who had to organise things and raise money. University teaching as a whole was placed under the supervision of a General Board of Studies. This latter body, from which the General Board of the Faculties developed after the major statutory changes of 1926, was not then of any great importance, mainly because so much of the undergraduate teaching (virtually all of it in the case of the long-established subjects like mathematics and classics) was in the hands of the Colleges. Indeed, the very idea of a General Board of Studies was accepted only reluctantly by the Senate in 1879; and the Master of Caius, in a splendidly vituperative sermon preached from the pulpit of Great St Mary's on Easter Day 1882 against the Statutory Commissioners sent down to Cambridge by the government of the day to amend University and College laws, included the institution of a General Board of Studies in his catalogue of injustices inflicted on the Colleges.[19]

It has already been implied by what has gone before that part of the complexity of Cambridge derives from the fact that it is also a University of Colleges. There were then seventeen of them, the oldest, Peterhouse, dating back to 1284, and the most recent, Downing College, founded in 1800. There was, in addition, Selwyn College (1882), which was technically not a College but had formal status within the University as a Public Hostel, a status intermediate between the existing Colleges and Private Hostels for which separate provision was made in the Statutes. In effect a Public Hostel functioned as a College and students living there had the same privileges and obligations as if they were members of one of the seventeen Colleges. The Colleges were, as they still are, corporate bodies distinct from the corporate body that formed the University. Again, it is difficult to better the description of them given in the early editions of the *Student's Handbook*: 'They possess and manage their own property; they are self-governing and elect their own officers, and for nearly all purposes they are

[18] *Reporter 1898–9*, 880–1.   [19] D. A. Winstanley, *Later Victorian Cambridge* (Cambridge, 1947), 358.

independent of University control.' The University existed before the Colleges, for it rose to importance in the first half of the thirteenth century, whereas the oldest College was not founded until the end of that century;

> yet nevertheless it is almost impossible now to conceive of the University apart from the Colleges, for the connexion between them is of the most intimate kind. The University is in part supported by contributions from the Colleges; certain officers of Colleges have special privileges in the University, and some Professors of the University are entitled to certain privileges and emoluments in the Colleges; and without any formal agreement to that effect the University and the Colleges do as a matter of fact recognise each other's regulations. This intimacy of connexion is explained by the fact that nearly all the members of the University belong to the Colleges, and that all the members of the Colleges belong to the University. Thus the same persons acting in different capacities manage the business of the Colleges and the business of the University, and so the good understanding which makes this dual organisation possible is maintained easily and without an effort.[20]

'Easily and without an effort.' Well, that may have been the acceptable thing to tell the undergraduates; but it was a gross simplification of the intricate political world of Cambridge, to which Cornford sought to provide a guide. The story goes that once a visitor stopped a don in the courts of one of the Colleges 'and asked "Excuse me, sir, but would you tell me how this University is governed?" The extraordinary suddenness of the question shook the truth out of the unwary victim, and before he knew what he was doing, he ejaculated "Very badly," and was gone before the questioner had time to recover from his surprise.'[21] But in fact, although potentially baffling to the outsider, the University had a remarkably effective form of government. Moreover, it was one which in essence was extremely democratic – or perhaps more accurately, as Cornford has it, aristo-democratic – involving extensive consultation and, ultimately, requiring a high level of agreement on what should be done before it could be done. It was not, therefore, a system of government in which policy was made actively and applied, but one where decisions were implemented by consent or were tolerated when the various parties recognised that they could no longer be expediently opposed.

The resident senior members were the *de facto* governing body of the University, conducting their own business according to their own rules, though, as we shall see, on occasion there could be effective intervention in University affairs by the members of the Senate at large. The resident dons constituted a political society which was small enough for everyone to know, or to know of, everyone else. Cambridge had about it something of the cosiness (and also, no doubt, the claustrophobia) of village life, a quality enhanced by the connexions of kin that also bound the dons together. Much of

[20] *Handbook*, 5.   [21] *CR*, 5 June 1907, 474.

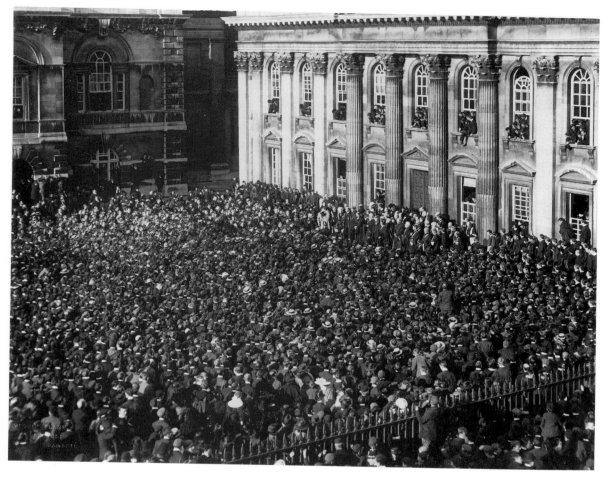

5   The Proclamation of His Majesty King Edward VII, 25 January 1901. The Senate-House Yard fulfilling its role as the University's village green, where members could gather for the formal celebration of major public events.

their business would be the topic of conversation in College, at dinner, at casual meetings before and after lectures and seminars, or in the laboratories and in the Library, or simply in passing on the street. No doubt in the course of these conversations, alongside purely rational exchanges, in which problems would be analysed and propositions sorted logically, other more intuitive and instinctive personal responses would come into play. Not 'what the issues are', but 'who supports whom, or what, and why?', would enter into consideration as a don made up his mind. Some order was given to the progress of important items of business by having it discussed in one or other of the many specialist committees appointed and stocked by the resident dons mainly from among themselves. Committees notoriously take on a life of their own, and here again questions of personality as much as rational consideration of given issues would play a part. In due course, members of a committee would arrive at a consensus (or sometimes agree to differ), and would write down their conclusions in the form of minutes or reports for circulation to the larger community. Such conclusions then become the subject of further and extensive consultation, some informal (as part of the general gossip of the place), some formal (as when a Report from a Board or Syndicate might be the subject of a Discussion of the Senate). On many occasions after wider deliberation matters would be referred back to the originating body for re-consideration and re-formulation.[22]

In order to become binding on the whole society, decisions about communal business were made formally at Congregations of the Senate, actually held in the Senate-House: but it was only necessary for a handful of members of the Senate to be present for a valid decision to be made. When a decision to make a change in the University was to be made, or someone was to be appointed to office, or to a committee, or to examine, or proposed for a degree then 'the proposal is embodied in as short a sentence as can grammatically be managed by the Council of the Senate, and is called a Grace'. At a Congregation,

> there sits the Vice-Chancellor on a gilded chair in the centre of the dais, wearing his cap and a splendid gown ... On his left stand two men draped mysteriously with hoods folded as no other man has them. You can hear one of them reading from a paper, and see him take his cap off at the end of every sentence, while his colleague tries to keep pace with him and is generally only a decimal of a second behind him in getting his cap off and on again. Nobody else seems to listen to the reader at all. They are the Proctors; and it is the Senior Proctor who is reading the Graces – lots and lots of them, as fast as he can, and at every full stop he says *Placet* under his breath, and raises his cap and gallops off again.[23]

But, in the more austere language of the University *Ordinances*, 'any member of the Senate who objects to any Grace or Supplicat may signify his opposition by pronouncing the words *non placet* immediately after such Grace or Supplicat has been read'.[24]

When this happened, 'confusion seems let loose. Everybody is in motion.'[25] For, to quote the ordinance again,

> The Senate-House shall be completely cleared from the West end as far Eastwards as may be necessary of persons who are not members of the Senate: and the members of the Senate present who desire to vote shall take their seats, if they are in favour of the Grace or

22 For an analysis of this type of political society see Peter Laslett, 'The Face to Face Society', in Peter Laslett (ed.), *Philosophy, Politics and Society* (Oxford, 1956; reprinted 1970), 157–84.
23 *CR*, 5 June 1907, 474.
24 *Ordinances 1908*, 268. *Placet* – 'it pleases', from the Latin *placere*, to please. Hence *non placet* – it does not please.
25 *CR*, 5 June 1907, 474.

Supplicat just read, on the South side of the Senate-House; if opposed to it, on the North side.

If in the opinion of both the Proctors the result of such a division was obvious, then the Senior Proctor might declare the result immediately without taking votes singly; but any two members of the Senate could ask the Vice-Chancellor to take the votes singly.[26] In that case, each voter had to write on a card ('The Council are of opinion that the writing on the cards may be either in ink or in pencil; and they have not specified the kind of card on which the votes should be recorded')[27] his name, degree and college, and either 'the word *placet* or the words *non placet* (as his vote may be)'. Those who were in favour of the Grace would then proceed up the South side of the Senate-House and hand in their card, marked placet, to the Senior Proctor or the Senior Pro-Proctor who would be waiting at the foot of the dais to receive it, returning to their place by walking down the centre of the room; for those voting non-placet, the process was repeated on the North side of the Senate-House and their cards were collected by the Junior Proctor, and the Junior Pro-Proctor. The votes were counted at the time, and the Vice-Chancellor announced the result. Subsequently, details of who voted, and how they cast their vote, might be published: it would certainly become known.[28]

Acute observers of this very open and public political system noted that it had certain curious characteristics. The first was that, by and large, the number of residents who actually participated in votes in the Senate-House, except on quite rare and special occasions, was a relatively small proportion of those entitled to do so. It was unusual to muster more than a hundred or so even when there had been a flurry of controversy about a particular matter. Indeed, this was in some respects fortunate since the Senate-House itself was incapable of accommodating all the resident members of the Senate at the same time. Further, a still smaller proportion of dons took a regular interest or an active part in University affairs generally; though most would be stirred into action when their own interests were at stake. By 1901, there were already complaints that the forty-one or so major University bodies contained, in arithmetical terms, some 600 places, roughly the number of resident dons. But the burden of work on these bodies ('voluntary and unpaid' besides involvement in 'the affairs of the Colleges, which occupy a large and additional amount of leisure') fell unevenly. The 600 places were not occupied by different people, for 'they are really a stage army, the same names repeatedly recurring. One name, for instance, we find no fewer than twelve times.'[29] Potentially, this might have concentrated influence in the hands of a

---

[26] *Ordinances* 1908, 268–9.   [27] *Ibid.*, 271.   [28] *Ibid.*

[29] *CR*, 9 May 1901, 293. The same is true today. A cursory glance at 'University Officers: Members of University Bodies: Representatives of the University', *Reporter*, 9 October 1990, reveals that a single person could be listed as serving, at the same time, on no fewer than thirty-four major University committees of various kinds.

few, but the various bodies had eventually to bring their proposals to the whole community for ratification. That proved a powerful constraint on change, and tended to favour the *status quo*, however much a change was needed or thought desirable. As Dr Alex Hill, the Master of Downing, perceptively remarked in October 1898 of his previous year as Vice-Chancellor,

> Changes in the organization of the studies of the University have been but few. Certain proposals have been made by Boards and Syndicates, but rejected by the Senate; shewing that the system of legislation by *referendum*, upon which the government of the University is based, is a guarantee against any rapid or extensive changes in its organic life. Its development is likely to be in the future, as in the past, a gradual process.[30]

But other consequences followed, for in politics all is not necessarily as it seems. Intelligent people, thwarted in what they wanted to do by the constitutional form of the system, would try to find ways of achieving their end despite it. Often the prospect of new resources for a new development, even if not quite sufficient (for such matters were always the subject of hard bargaining), would be enough to reconcile opinion to it. Or perhaps some particular initiative might be run alongside and not technically as part of the University: as we shall see, the education of women at Cambridge in this period fell into this category. But for most purposes, in order to make the constitution work, the dons must play politics. Whether to stop things happening, or whether to get things done, the dons had to engage with each other in a sport as ancient as society itself. In the pursuit of influence and power, the academic behaved much like any other kind of politician. Colleagues had to be persuaded and manipulated, rewarded, bought off or punished. Some of the rules for all of this were quite explicit; but many were unspoken and implied. Moreover, the would-be academic politician had to recognise that colleagues would not be moved by reason: ways had to be found to work on prejudice and to appeal to baser instincts like fear and self-interest. Passions were involved; success in the play was often accompanied by wit and fun; but malice and bitterness were part of it also. The game never ceased and the myriad small exchanges of daily life were an integral part of it. And the notorious ability of the donnish mind to be led by logic from the reasonable to the fantastic, to be open-minded and see all sides of an issue, yet be capable of advancing with a fine line of polemic from any particular perspective, and to be excessively secretive about its real beliefs, made the imposition of party discipline next to impossible. Cornford, as a young Master of Arts, confronted *The Academic Dilemma:*[31]

> If one and one made only one,
> There might be something to be done.

[30] *Reporter* 1898–9, 8.　　[31] *CR*, 22 January 1903, 134.

But what on earth am I to do,
If they persist in making two?

Two stupid parties alternate
In ruling this distracted state.

One sits on this side, one on that:
The floor between is bare and flat.

Why mayn't I sit upon the floor?
To choose a side is such a bore!

To sit on *this* might seem polemic
And anything but academic.

But then again, to sit on *that*,
I'd also have to bell the cat.

I don't see how, upon my oath,
I could contrive to sit on both.

The course most academical
Was simply not to sit at all.

Besides, this education talk
Was really hardly worth the walk.

(*Note.* 'Academic' 's Greek. Translation:-
'Indifferent to Education')

Imagine what surprise was mine,
When someone breathed the word 'Resign.'

To Be is just as bad, or good,
As Not to Be: I said I would.

But then uprose my friend Sir Bill;
Followed Sir John; and then Sir Phil.

No academic types were they;
But they had 'views,' like things of clay.

I could not stand that party lot:
I wrote and said that I would *not*.

But when they said, 'You said you would,'
My answer was: 'Oh, very good!'

Dilemmas are a forte of mine:
I'll both resign and not resign.

I'll ask the electors which they like —
A partisan, or Neutral Mike.

To solve that horrid party bother,
I'll be first one and then the other.

San Remo is from Remus named:
He jumped the wall – and was he blamed?

The others needn't take offence, if
They *do* look somewhat inexpensive.

                    Moral

Not every child that's born alive
Is liberal or conservative.

Add both together, and they give –
Academic Representative.

Subtract them both, and you will see
Political Nonentity.

As the nineteenth century drew to a close, there were still certain issues which deeply moved and divided the University community. Among those which roused most emotion were the continuing close association of Cambridge with the established Church of England and the attempts made to secure a University education at Cambridge for women. The late Victorians were also torn between the increasing demands made of the University to teach undergraduates and the desire to move forward into new areas of scholarship and research. But teaching did not stand still and there were constant pressures to provide new courses and to change the content of old ones. Everyone had his own view as to what it was suitable to teach the young; and cynics would say that some opinions were determined by the need to keep up income from student fees and by the existence of old sets of lecture-notes. New Triposes had a tough fight to gain admission to the University. Even more fierce were the battles to reform the well-established courses in Mathematics and Classics. The development of new subjects and the promotion of research had implications for funding. Sometimes a College or a benefactor would achieve a radical shift in the course of scholarship by stealth or donation; but more generally, more money had to be found. It was inconceivable that the great institutions which made up the University should become clients of the State; and Cambridge was not a large or thriving town populated by newly rich bankers and manufacturers willing to endow great civic educational enterprises. Thus as the new century dawned some of the politics of academia turned on the quest for funds.

The influence of the Church of England was still very strong in late nineteenth-century Cambridge. On over forty occasions during the year an Anglican preacher, often of great distinction, delivered a sermon 'before the University' in Great St Mary's Church. The sermon would be attended by the principal University officers and Heads of Houses, who would walk in procession from the Senate-House to their assigned seats in the Church. Despite movement for change from within the University, backed by powerful political interference from without, Cambridge still seemed essentially part of the Anglican establishment, and even in the early twentieth century a natural and unremarkable ladder of preferment was from don to Dean or Bishop. A succession of Royal Commissions and Acts of Parliament had forced open Oxford and Cambridge to students who were not members of the Church of England and had allowed them to take the BA degree; but religious tests for higher degrees and membership of the University's governing body were not fully removed until 1871. Even so, it was left to Statutory Commissioners in 1881–2 to redraw College Statutes lifting religious and celibate qualifications for appointment to nearly all Fellowships and Headships. (An exception was the Mastership of St Catharine's College, which until 1927 was attached to a Canonry at Norwich; and two-thirds of the Fellows of Queens' were required to find a layman as their President, while a simple majority would secure the election of a Priest.)[32]

But the founding of a new College restricted to Anglicans and intended 'to encourage in its students simplicity of living and to develop in them the Christian character' seemed to some radicals a defiant gesture by supporters of the Church of England against the abandonment of Anglican religious qualifications for membership of the University. The new foundation was a memorial to George Augustus Selwyn, a great missionary and the first Bishop of New Zealand. It cannot have escaped notice that, as Bishop of Lichfield, Selwyn had campaigned vigorously against the repeal of the Test Acts in the House of Lords; but even more its opponents argued that the foundation of Selwyn as a 'sectarian' College was to be deplored because it offended against two principles which were essential to the very ideal of a modern University: the broadest religious toleration and thorough intellectual freedom.[33] Conservative opinion, however, held the day. The College was opened with great ceremony on 10 October 1882, when the Revd the Hon. A. T. Lyttelton of Trinity College (whose mother's sister was Mrs Gladstone) was installed as Master. Seven Bishops and almost all the senior clergymen holding University or College office were present for the ceremonies. At luncheon, the Vice-Chancellor made reference to the controversy surrounding the memorial to Bishop Selwyn, but he believed that those Liberals

[32] The activities of the Parliamentary Commissioners are dealt with very thoroughly by Winstanley, *Later Victorian Cambridge*, 263–359. John Baker kindly gave me extra information about the Master of St Catharine's College.
[33] *CR*, 22 March 1882, 244–5.

6   Bishop Charles John Abraham (on the right) at the laying of the foundation
stone of Selwyn College Chapel, 15 June 1893. Abraham had been George
Augustus Selwyn's suffragan bishop both in New Zealand and afterwards at
Lichfield. He was secretary to the Selwyn Memorial Committee and the
founding of the College owed much to his initiative and drive. The Chapel was
consecrated on St Etheldreda's day, 17 October, 1895. The architect was Sir
Arthur Blomfield, and the carvings on the stalls include impish heads of John
Morley, Lord Salisbury, Sir William Harcourt and other politicians prominent
in the general election campaign of 1895. The Hon. Arthur Lyttelton, Master,
stands behind the stone. This was his last day as Master. His successor, Bishop
John Selwyn, son of George Augustus, stands eighth from the left, on crutches.

opposed to the College should tolerate the new foundation. 'He would admit that in
his opinion the best possible academic education was given in any one of the old
colleges where persons of all creeds mixed on a social equality.' But he recognised the
right of any persons to found colleges with particular religious aims and that such
institutions might well apply to be

admitted into fellowship with the other colleges. He thought it would be an admission
which the University would be extremely illiberal in refusing. In his public capacity, as

well as in his private capacity, as a member of the Senate, he should do everything he could to give the students of Selwyn College a recognised position amongst the colleges of the University.[34]

On 8 February 1883 a Grace was passed duly recognising the College as a 'Public Hostel'.[35] Under the skilled guidance of its first Masters (Lyttelton was succeeded by Bishop Selwyn's own son, retired from the see of Melanesia, and then by Alexander Kirkpatrick, the distinguished Regius Professor of Hebrew, later Dean of Ely), and in recognition of the self-sacrifice and dedication of its early dons, the College gradually gained acceptance as part of the University community.

But the University's religious tolerance did not stretch far beyond the Anglican fold. An attempt was made in 1898 to gain for St Edmund's House University status as a Public Hostel. The Duke of Norfolk was the chief patron of St Edmund's, the object of which was 'to found, establish, maintain and conduct a Hostel for Students . . . in or near Cambridge, in which men who are destined for the secular priesthood of the Catholic Church in communion with the See of Rome, may be educated as Members of the University of Cambridge'.[36] Money had been raised, land and a freehold bought, and there were at the time seven students in residence (coming under the category of non-collegiate students and living in a Private Hostel), all reading for honours. As the Censor for the non-collegiate students said, these young men 'took part in the interests and sports of the ordinary undergraduates . . . they were only under stricter discipline than other students'.[37] Similar arguments were advanced to those justifying the establishment of Selwyn College: Cambridge ought to be able to accommodate those who had particular social needs. But again, the anti-church radicals objected that the proposal was inimical to the spirit of a modern University and it was contrary to the intention of all the Parliamentary legislation designed to break down religious barriers at the old Universities. Some, of whom Henry Jackson was one, argued at the Discussion that 'since the object of the Test Act was to break down the exclusive character of the University, it would be fulfilled rather than frustrated by admitting persons, who otherwise would lose the advantage of a University education'. This view was supported by Dr Verrall who said that he 'had never understood liberalism to mean the prohibition of illiberal experiments'. J. M. E. McTaggart, the Trinity philosopher, however, argued fiercely that there was no question of fairness to Roman Catholics involved; 'that Selwyn was no precedent, and if it were we need not follow it; that because a mistake was then made, there was no reason for repeating it; that after all St Edmund's House was only a technical school and the University ought not to recognise it'. And, despite the voices in favour from, among others, the Master of

[34] Ibid., 18 October 1882, 26–7.   [35] Reporter 1882–3, 367.   [36] Ibid., 1897–8, 504.
[37] Ibid., 585.

Trinity and the Provost of King's, the Senate refused St Edmund's the recognition it desired. The debate at the Discussion had been lengthy and it appeared that the 'weight of the speakers was certainly on the side of accepting the grace' the numbers voting and the majority against the Grace (218 placet, 471 non-placet), was at first surprising. Although Jackson had professed not to hear so much a 'no-Popery cry, but a no-Popery mutter', it would seem that a combination of the anti-religious and conservative Anglicans in the Senate proved to be a formidable political alignment.[38]

In the debate about St Edmund's, the Provost of King's had pointed out that the old Colleges still had to make arrangements for Church of England services and that in Cambridge generally the Anglicans had a distinct advantage. Nowhere did this show more clearly than in the continued compulsion for undergraduates to attend services in College chapels. This had long been a contentious issue: as far back as 1834 there had been controversy when Christopher Wordsworth, the Master of Trinity, had deprived Connop Thirlwall of his Assistant Tutorship because Thirlwall had attacked the rule of compulsory chapel attendance in a pamphlet arguing that the Colleges were not religious seminaries. He had remarked that 'the constant repetition of a heartless, mechanical service' was a positive evil in fostering true faith, and that 'our daily services might be omitted altogether without any material detriment to religion', since the majority of those who came did so unwillingly, and the few who came in a spirit of piety found the services unedifying and of little spiritual value.[39] There is some evidence that occasionally the undergraduates rebelled about regular attendance at chapel, or sought revenge by publishing registers of the non-attendance of the dons. But by and large, the custom seems to have been observed with remarkably little breach throughout the century. No doubt when once the dissenters began to gain admission to the University in fair number, and it was not uncommon for others to confess to a loss of faith altogether, it might have been assumed that compulsory attendance might not last for ever. But we know that, at Trinity at least, those who did not wish to go to chapel had formally to be excused, and, if they were of Anglican background, had to seek their parents' consent in writing.[40] In November 1904, Cornford circulated a pamphlet to his colleagues giving notice of a resolution for the Annual College Meeting the following January 'That it is desirable that it should no longer be part of the duty of officers of the College to put pressure of any sort upon members of the College to attend the services in the Chapel.'[41]

[38] *CR*, 10 March 1898, 270–1, 334; *Reporter* 1897–8, 504–5, 584–91, 825.
[39] The story is well told in D. A. Winstanley, *Early Victorian Cambridge* (Cambridge, 1940), 73–8.
[40] Christopher N. L. Brooke, *A History of the University of Cambridge*, vol. IV: *1870–1990* (Cambridge, 1993), 117.
[41] Cornford, 'Compulsory Chapel', 1. A copy of Cornford's pamphlet is in the University Library: Cam. c. 904. 14.

In support of his resolution, Cornford argued that the idea of compulsory chapel attendance was both fundamentally irreligious and incompatible with the ideal of a place of education and research. He recognised that 'The custom which I seek to abolish has been allowed to continue untouched by generations of men, among whom I recognise many spiritual and intellectual superiors' and he disclaimed any notion that he himself might claim 'a finer sense than they of the meaning of religion'. He could see that the custom was explicable by history: 'It is the last survival from the days when every member of the University who refused to profess adhesion to the Christian faith was subject to persecution. In contrast with the disabilities inflicted on the unbeliever before the abolition of tests, the small remnant of disciplinary persecution involved in "compulsory" attendance at Chapel may well have seemed trifling.' He could also see that its maintenance 'wore the attractive aspect of a compromise', and the 'custom once established, I am driven to suppose that those who have thought about it seriously enough to perceive its objectionable character have felt that the time was not ripe for the attempt to abolish it. So it has continued unchallenged.'

This was no longer good enough. 'The practice of our own College appears to be', he wrote,

> that undergraduates who are not members of the Anglican communion are expected to make a declaration to that effect. Those who do not make such a declaration are informed that they must be present in the College Chapel at two services on Sundays and two on week-days. If they absent themselves, they are liable to certain petty penalties on the same scale as those which are inflicted for trivial breaches of discipline.

If such a regulation were to be introduced now for the first time, he went on, 'the very men whose office it has been to carry it out would have been the first to see how irreligious it is'. The worship of God was a most solemn and awful matter, and those who had a responsibility for the spiritual life of young men must surely set it before them in a serious light. Thus it

> seems clear to me that we are failing in our duty when we make it a matter of discipline, and put absence from Christian worship on the same level in our scale of punishments with staying out too late at night or making a noise in the court ... How any religiously-minded man can view with complacence a congregation of men, nominally assembled for the worship of God, of whom some are present *because* they would be punished if they were not, is a thing that I cannot understand.

The custom trivialised religion and demeaned it in the eyes of the young. Cornford had even

> heard of a boat's crew being sent to morning chapel in order to ensure their being out of bed by a certain hour during the period of training for a race. The story may not be true; but the fact that it could be told in Cambridge without apparently exciting disapproval

shows to what depths of spiritual degradation the system of compulsory religion may lead.[42]

But Cornford had a second set of arguments against compulsory chapel. His ideal of a University demanded 'an absolute impartiality towards all matters of speculation'. He did not object to the teaching of theological and cosmological dogma, nor to the idea that the College Chapel might be afforded a 'unique opportunity of recommending' the 'select doctrines of a single church'. However, the attendance of undergraduates should not be forced on such occasions.

> As private individuals, we are all at liberty to express and to act upon our own religious opinions and, with a due sense of responsibility, to influence, if we can, the opinions and practice of others. What is objectionable is that it should be the regular duty of college officials to represent to young men, fresh from school and anxious to be on good terms with the new authorities, that religious observance is identical with the observance of a college rule. To do so is to create the impression that certain opinions on speculative matters are specially favoured here, and that conformity is orderly and respectable. I think that it must be agreed that this use of authority is inconsistent with the strict official impartiality towards all theoretical beliefs which it is the first duty of a body of men engaged in advanced education and in the pursuit of truth.

He stressed that 'we cannot strengthen character or deepen spiritual life by relieving men from the necessity of making moral decisions for themselves', and ended his pamphlet with

> The pious builders of our chapel quaintly inscribed upon its eastern front an unfinished legend. The words of it were used by Jesus when he made a scourge of small cords to purify the Temple of God of an abuse which some might think a less outrage upon religion than the abuse of Christian worship for purposes of discipline. If the sentence were completed thus: 'My house shall be called the house of prayer, but ye have made it a place of detention,' I do not know what answer we should dare to make.[43]

Cornford's challenge was taken up by Russell Kerr Gaye, who had won the Porson Prize in 1898, been Chancellor's Classical Medallist in 1900 and elected to a Fellowship in October 1901. He agreed with his colleague that the matter was one of the first importance, and he had read Cornford's paper 'carefully and with the deepest interest'. But he could not agree with it. There had clearly been some discussion in the College that a reform of chapel-going might have consequences for the material prosperity of the College, either in depriving it of pupils or of benefactions (this is not, in fact, raised in Cornford's pamphlet), and on this matter Gaye did not feel qualified to speak,

---

[42] *Ibid.*, 2–4.   [43] *Ibid.*, 5–6.

although he did recognise that the effect any change in the rule might have on the outside world 'ought not to be left entirely out of account'. But Gaye's main point of attack was that Cornford had not substantiated his argument that compulsory chapel-going was irreligious. Gaye accepted that compulsion in the abstract was not necessarily a desirable thing; 'But it seems to me that Mr Cornford in his over-earnest enthusiasm for the ideal has lost sight of the more practical problems which we are here called upon to face: and he has thus been led to advocate a reform for which the time is certainly not yet.'

The trouble was, that Cornford 'seems to assume, though he does not explicitly say so', that the young undergraduate came up to Cambridge 'fully capable of forming a carefully reasoned conclusion on a serious matter of this kind; that he is capable in fact of conscientiously deciding for himself whether he ought to attend Chapel or not'. Now some young men might be in this state; but their number was comparatively small. If there were those who could explain properly why they did not wish to attend chapel, then there was no hardship to them, surely, to have to be able to explain matters to the Dean; and the Dean, if he was really satisfied by their arguments, would, of course, excuse them from attending. The fact remained, however, 'that under our present system of public school education a boy who has just left school certainly does not, as a general rule, possess a sufficient sense of responsibility to justify the College authorities in allowing him unlimited freedom in this matter'. And Cornford's proposed reform, far from making the youth more truly self-reliant, would instead create in his mind 'an irresponsible attitude towards the serious side of life that could hardly fail to be pernicious'. Young Anglicans had been used to attending chapel at school; they needed to continue to attend at College. The most effectual way of educating a young mind in the ways of religion was to secure attendance at chapel, just as the best way of teaching him his academical subject was to require his attendance at lectures and classes (theoretically as objectionable). Gaye continued by admitting that 'with much that is commonly accepted and taught in the name of Christianity I cannot myself agree: but of the unique value of its teaching as a whole I have no doubt whatsoever'. Therefore it should be preserved intact and the College would 'not be justified in relaxing further the not very burdensome rules which at present regulate the attendance of undergraduates at the services in the College Chapel'. The culmination of Gaye's argument was that he was as anxious as Cornford to realise the ideal situation, indeed in respect 'of the end to be desired I do not think . . . that there is any very material difference between our opinions'; but Cornford had exaggerated the evils of the present situation and the 'purely destructive policy' he seemed to favour would result 'only in disaster'. In short, the 'continuance of the present system with all its faults is at least preferable to the sudden establishment of religious or irreligious anarchy: and before we resolve to break down an existing institution such as that which is now threatened, we ought to have some clear notion of what we are going to set up in its place'.[44]

Gaye's pamphlet *contra*-Cornford is a classic example of donnish political debate, boxing round the main issues, skilfully minimising the real differences of opinion between himself and his opponent, while at the same time insinuating that he was a rash and inconsiderate reformer and implying that he lacked practical experience and therefore could not be trusted. Although Gaye's pamphlet is in almost every respect inferior in style, tone and content to Cornford's original essay, it would appear that he carried the Fellowship with him. Although the College Council agreed that they would not impose penalties on those who failed to attend chapel, a notice was circulated to say that students who were members of the Church of England 'are expected to attend Divine Service in chapel, on Sundays both at Morning and Evening Prayers and on weekdays twice in the week'. There remained an ambiguity about the meaning of 'expected', and in 1913 the Tutors proposed it be clarified to 'required' with the concession that attendance only once on Sundays would be necessary and that those 'who profess a conscientious objection to attendance' would be excused. At a special College Meeting in November, 'after various manoeuvres, it was resolved, on the motion of Henry Jackson, himself a fervent believer, seconded by the eminent agnostic McTaggart, "That attendance at the College Chapel be not enforced by gating or other penalty." From then on, chapel was no longer in any sense compulsory.'[45]

Cornford himself continued his campaign, and, in a less cautious, more teeth-gnashing mood in a desolate place (actually in Trinity), he argued at a meeting of the Heretics in 1911 that a University 'ought to stand absolutely clear of all dogmatic systems'. A University had a duty to test all argument and all knowledge. By definition, this could not be done with religion. Cambridge had no business to maintain one creed rather than another, and, indeed, 'if they had an Anglican chapel, they ought also to have a mosque, a Hindu temple, a Baptist chapel and so on, with an official attached to each'. And as a parting shot, he ventured the view that the future of theology lay in taking its place as a branch of anthropology.[46]

[44] R. K. Gaye, 'To the Master and Fellows of Trinity College, Cambridge' (25 November 1904). Gaye's pamphlet is also in the University Library: Cam c. 904. 40.

[45] Brooke, *History of the University*, 117–18. Considerable moral pressure continued to be applied to the undergraduates. On 27 February 1914 the College Council was asked to approve the following statement for inclusion in the Tutors' circular: 'Divine service is celebrated daily in the College Chapel both in the morning and in the evening, except during certain periods in vacation of which due notice is given. The hours of service are specified on a circular issued at the beginning of each term. All members of the College are welcome at the services in Chapel; but attendance is in no case enforced by any penalty. Members of the Church of England are expected to attend, unless they shall have stated to their Tutor or to one of the Deans their wish to be excused.' An amendment was moved to omit the last sentence, but this was lost by 7 votes to 4, and the original motion was carried by 7 votes to 1. John Easterling kindly looked out this material for me.

[46] F. M. Cornford, 'Religion in the University' (reprinted for The Heretics, November 1911), 2, 3, 6.

If chapel-going touched one raw nerve in turn-of-the-century Cambridge, university education for women touched another. Pioneers in the cause of women's education had brought Girton College to Cambridge in 1869, and founded Newnham College in 1871. It was clearly hoped by some, though not by others, that the two women's Colleges would be associated with the University, and for ten years or so very informal arrangements were made, dependent solely on the good will of a number of individuals, to allow women students to attend certain classes and to have their examination papers set and marked. Others were persuaded that the liaison would be as temporary as it was informal, and that in due course, once the new Colleges were properly on their feet, they would become fully independent and belong to a separate University especially for women. However, in 1881, a little more formality was entered into. The Senate approved, by 398 votes to 32, a proposal that students at Girton and Newnham should be allowed to sit the regular Tripos examinations, that their results should be published separately but alongside those of the men and that they should obtain a certificate confirming how they had performed.[47]

In fact they did rather well – and by 1891 of 490 women who had sat honours examinations only 9 had failed to be classed.[48] In some subjects (like history and languages) their presence was quite significant, and by the end of the century the two Colleges between them usually had around 400 students in residence in any year. But there was no sign that they were going to set up as an independent university, and in 1896, in response to a flurry of memorials and correspondence in the press, a Syndicate was set up to consider on what conditions, and with what restrictions, if any, women might be admitted to degrees in the University. Miss B. A. Clough and Miss K. Jex-Blake had identified the disadvantages faced by 'women who study here under the conditions prescribed by the University' or by those 'who wish to devote themselves to learning and research after the prescribed course is over' as: restriction in the use of the University Library, exclusion from competition for University Prizes and Scholarships, exclusion from sending in dissertations and from advanced study, 'severance from the University' and 'precarious access' to University lectures and laboratories.[49]

The Syndicate took evidence and in March 1897 published a massive Report. Neither the advocates, nor the opponents, of including women in the University were to be satisfied by it. For a start, less than two-thirds of the Syndics signed the Report, and then no reason was given for the changes proposed – 'the members of Senate are presumably left to disinter these from the voluminous appendices which occupy 38 pages of the *Reporter*'.[50] Those who were in favour of moving towards a 'Mixed University' had wanted women to be awarded degrees on the same basis as those

[47] Brooke, *History of the University, 324.*   [48] *CR*, 20 May 1897, 364.   [49] *Ibid.*, 13 May 1897, 343.
[50] *Ibid.*, 4 March 1897, 266.

awarded to men, to have the right to attend lectures and laboratories, and to share in the endowments of the University. But practically none of these demands were contemplated by the Syndicate in their Report. The principal recommendation was 'That it is desirable that the title of the Degree of Bachelor of Arts be conferred by diploma upon women who, in accordance with the now existing Ordinances, shall hereafter satisfy the Examiners in a Final Tripos Examination and shall have kept by residence nine terms at least: provided that the title so conferred shall not involve membership of the University.' There were four other, largely consequential, recommendations: one allowing for the same privilege to be granted to suitably qualified past women students; another to allow, under the same terms, the award of the MA degree; the third to permit women to hold the titles of the degrees of Doctor in Science or Letters, if they had held the title of Master of Arts for five years and if they had 'made valuable and original contributions to Science or Letters'; and the fourth allowing women to receive, *honoris causa*, titles of degrees in arts, law, letters, science and music. None of the further recommendations, however, were to be put to the Senate unless the first one was approved.[51] Stripped of technicalities, what was being proposed was the title only of a degree, and for that a fee would be charged – unlike in the case of the equivalent 'honorary titles' of degrees for men. If the hope had been that this constituted a modest and moderate compromise which would win the support of the Senate, it was to be confounded.

There was nothing moderate or modest about the campaign which was launched against the Syndicate's proposals; and it is of some interest that the student-body became excited by them also. It would be tedious to rehearse all the arguments that were made against women in the summer of 1897; but among those who opposed the cause there was more than a whiff of paranoia and a sense of a society betrayed. It was not the women who had grievances, it was the members of the Senate 'who are anxious to maintain the ancient traditions of the University' who had the grievance. And 'this is a grievance precisely similar to that suffered by the burghers of an independent city of Ancient Greece, when a small party within the camp opened an unwatched postern to a body of revolutionists outside'. The Council had failed miserably in their duty when they had not consulted the Senate in 1870 about allowing examiners discretion to mark scripts for women. However, since 1881, the women had been given exactly what they had asked for – places in published class lists and formal certificates that they had gained those places. 'They have, therefore, no more ground of claim for further advantages than the labourers in the parable, who received each the penny he had agreed for.'[52] If they wanted degrees, then they should have gone to other Universities – after all London and Manchester awarded degrees to women. That a 'University for

[51] As quoted in *ibid.*, 6 May 1897, 322.   [52] J. H. Taylor in *ibid.*, 20 May 1897, 361.

Women' could not expect within a realistic time to attain the standing of Oxford and Cambridge was no justification for 'a proposal which endangers the continuance of the reputation which these Universities now enjoy'. Why, it might be argued: 'It is impossible that within any time to which it is reasonable to look forward any High School for Girls can rival the prestige of Eton or Winchester: therefore Eton and Winchester ought forthwith to be thrown open to girls. We hardly fancy that Etonians or Wykehamists in any great number would allow the cogency of this reasoning.'[53] There was more than a suspicion that women students came to Cambridge to find husbands, rather than to study. Oxford had not been properly consulted: if Cambridge embarked on this rash experiment, then 'We are creditably informed that the heads of several large schools have already determined . . . no longer to send their men to Cambridge.'[54] The compromise of 1881 had been a mistake; it was illogical and unjustified; the thing to do now was to stand firm against the whole idea of a 'Mixed University' and give notice that, from 1900, women would no longer be allowed to sit the Tripos examinations.[55]

When the first rumours of the establishment of the Syndicate had begun to circulate round the Colleges in 1896, the undergraduates had organised a poll among themselves. The result had shown that while 446 were in favour of degrees for women, 1,723 were against.[56] Once the Syndicate reported, a new committee of undergraduates got up a petition against the proposal. This time there were 2,137 hostile signatures collected and presented to the Vice-Chancellor. A daring 300 ventured an opinion in favour of women.[57] The Council determined that the Senate would be given an opportunity to vote on the proposals at a Congregation to be held on 21 May. The Vice-Chancellor announced that voting would be allowed throughout the afternoon; there was criticism that because the day was a Friday many Assistant Masters in the schools distant from Cambridge who might wish to vote would not be free to do so; there was suspicion that the small cabal within the University which was in favour of the reform was trying to swamp the hostile opinion of the majority of the residents by encouraging the non-residents to turn out in large number; on the other hand, the undergraduates engaged in lobbying for a 'non-placet' among their seniors at home and abroad exhausted the stock of post-cards held in the Cambridge Post Office, and new supplies had to be sent for to London; ominously, the *University Reporter*, which of course 'is absolutely impartial on this question' announced that the Congregation to be held on 21 May was a Congregation 'not for degrees'.[58]

The day of the vote was turned into a carnival. Undergraduates paraded the streets carrying placards proclaiming 'No Women', 'No Gowns for Girtonites', 'Non-plus the

[53] *Ibid.*, 362. [54] *Ibid.*, 363. [55] W. F. McMichael, in *ibid.*, 6 May 1897, 325–6.
[56] Quoted in *ibid.*, 4 March 1897, 266.
[57] *Ibid.*, 13 May 1897, 339. [58] *Ibid.*, 340.

Newnhamites', 'Frustrate the Feminine Fanatics'. Above the bookshop opposite the Senate-House

> swung a thing in 'rational' blue and pink upon a bicycle: Caius had its pair of guys, and Trinity Street a she-dummy in cap and gown with a golden pigtail. Less obtrusive and more funny were the quintet of gaudy 'Lecture Hats – Latest Designs,' hung out from a Caius window. These unaccustomed sights were accompanied by the usual tow-path harmonies of horns, rattles, and the *vox humana*, from the crowd of straw hats on King's Parade.

But the MAs needed no intimidation. The Senior Proctor read out the Grace at one o'clock, and it was received with numerous shouts of 'non-placet'. Dr Montagu Butler, the Master of Trinity, who had married Agnata Ramsay, the best classical scholar in the Tripos of 1887, was among the first to emerge from the placet door; and he was followed by many of the most illustrious names in Cambridge. But the result was a foregone conclusion: the placet stream was decidedly thin, while the non-placets surged in their torrents. The Vice-Chancellor declared the result: 661 placet, 1,707 non-placet and Cambridge erupted into scenes of hilarious joy.[59]

In fact, when a close scrutiny of the vote was made, only 149 of the residents had voted for the proposal, 320 against. The dons at the heart of the University were as conservative and unmoveable on this matter as the MAs dispersed across the country in schools and parsonages and inns of court.[60] A further attempt to admit women to degrees was made in 1921, but it met with a similar result: rather surprising in view of the rapidly changing attitudes towards women in the first twenty years of the century; but perhaps this second vote against women may partly be explained by the fact that many of those who were undergraduate demonstrators in 1897 were voters in the Senate after the War.[61] Even though many of the most distinguished dons of late Victorian and Edwardian Cambridge worked hard for the cause of women's education, a clear majority was implacably opposed to the development of Cambridge as a 'Mixed University'. It was an emotional matter; it was, from a later perspective, ungenerous, ungracious and unjust; it was unfair to the women and the circumstances of the defeat in 1897 must have been humiliating to those members of the Senate who saw the proposal to allow the titles of degrees as a modest step in the right direction. But there was also a sense in which this ritual humiliation did not really matter: Girton and Newnham went from strength to strength. Some dons persisted in being difficult about women in their classrooms, but many more welcomed them. Their scholarship

[59] *Ibid.*, 27 May 1897, 374–5.
[60] *Ibid.* The *Cambridge Review* also published a special supplement on 3 June 1897 giving details of the voting.
[61] Again in 1921 undergraduate opinion was strongly against women becoming members of the University. Oxford, however, managed to do better in this respect and during 1920–1 argued the matter out and voted to admit women to the University. Brooke, *History of the University*, 325–7.

7   The vote on the admission of women to the titles of degrees, 21 May 1897:
the scene looking south at the end of Trinity Street outside Macmillan and
Bowes bookshop (now the Cambridge University Press bookshop). Great St
Mary's Church is in the background.

8   The declaration of the result of the ballot on the admission of women to the
titles of degrees, 21 May 1897.

was well regarded, and the two Colleges developed traditions at once individual and
distinct, but then also converging with all the others. Generations of women students
were only *technically* not members of the University, and the Senior Combination
Rooms of Girton and Newnham held their own with the best of the men's Colleges. By
the time that the members of the Senate had overcome their fear of the women, and
realised that they had been in reality a part of the University for decades, there was no
longer any need to pretend that they were being kept out: so in 1947 the women were
admitted to full membership without a vote being called for.[62] Of course, by then, the
dons knew that something ought to be done, only not anything that actually needed
doing at the time, but something which had not been done fifty years earlier.

Throughout these years there was no shortage of those who looked on the gloomy side
and became convinced that Cambridge could not possibly reform itself. Prejudice
acted as a restraint on the introduction of new courses and vested interests stood in the
way of reform of the old; lack of resources inhibited the development of both. But

[62] *Reporter* 1946–7, 1083–6; *ibid.*, 1947–8, 295–6, 398.

there was a paradox: Cambridge as a whole could not be said to be without wealth; so it was likely that poor management bedevilled university affairs and selfishness prevented an efficient use of college resources. In 1879, Arnold recalled nearly thirty years later,

> the air of Cambridge was full of schemes of University reform . . . A Royal Commission was on the point of issuing its report, and, with a youthful optimism which the result did not justify, we looked forward to seeing in the conclusions of the eminent men who formed the Commission the foundations laid for the growth of a new and greater Cambridge. The kernel of the whole question was the problem of University finance. Then, as now, Cambridge owned in the aggregate princely revenues, and was at the same time compelled to a beggarly penuriousness in all those matters which most concerned its welfare. The official revenues of the University and its Colleges were reckoned at £300,000 a year: the additional private expenditure of its members probably amounted to double that sum. Yet this University, claiming to be one of the two real Universities of the United Kingdom, had not (and still has not) any professors of the language and literature of the two greatest nations of Europe; its library was barely worthy of the middle ages; it was even without lecture rooms for its professors; worse than all, it did not really feel the need of any of these things.[63]

But there was another side to the medal: turn it over and it was clear that the case was overstated. Much had been achieved, even before the 1880s. Within the space of half a century new honours courses had been established in moral sciences (philosophy), natural sciences, theology, history, oriental languages, medieval and modern languages, mechanical sciences (engineering) and economics and politics. These supplemented the old staples of mathematics and classics, and revivified courses in law and medicine. What was just as surprising was the degree to which change had been generated in response to wider social and economic demands. Many of the new courses were strongly vocational in intent; this was certainly true of some of the languages, let alone the sciences and engineering. It had been the growing need for more medical doctors that had stimulated the demand for chemistry and biology, as well as promoting physiology and anatomy. Moreover, the new honours courses were popular and by the beginning of the new century a third of the University's graduates in honours took their degrees by way of the Natural or Mechanical Sciences Triposes. In addition many 'after graduating in mathematics, remain at the University to go through a further period of scientific study'.[64] By the turn of the century, the University was keen to develop agriculture, and public health; and there was a determined effort to have a hand in the training of school-teachers. Some of these subjects involved the University with the world outside: politics had to be transacted

---

[63] *CR*, 21 February 1907, 261.   [64] Letter by 'Vindex' in the *Times*, 30 October 1905, 4.

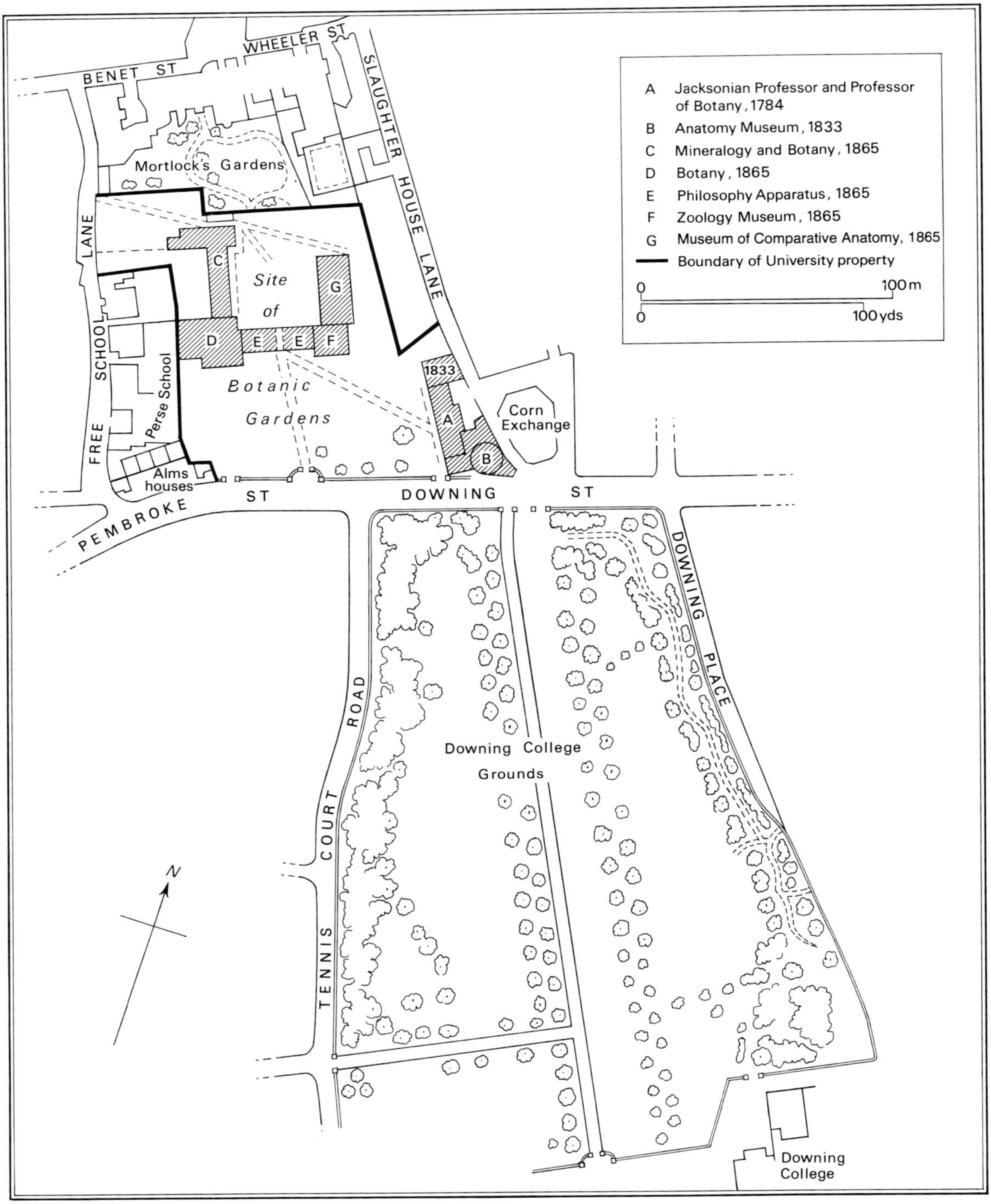

A Jacksonian Professor and Professor of Botany, 1784
B Anatomy Museum, 1833
C Mineralogy and Botany, 1865
D Botany, 1865
E Philosophy Apparatus, 1865
F Zoology Museum, 1865
G Museum of Comparative Anatomy, 1865
Boundary of University property
0
100m
0
100yds
BENET ST
WHEELER ST
SLAUGHTER HOUSE LANE
Mortlock's Gardens
Site of
Botanic Gardens
1833
Corn Exchange
FREE SCHOOL LANE
Perse School
Alms houses
PEMBROKE ST
DOWNING ST
DOWNING PLACE
TENNIS COURT ROAD
Downing College Grounds
Downing College
N

9 The Caves of Adullam: plan of the New Museums and Downing sites showing the growth of Cambridge
Development by 1865

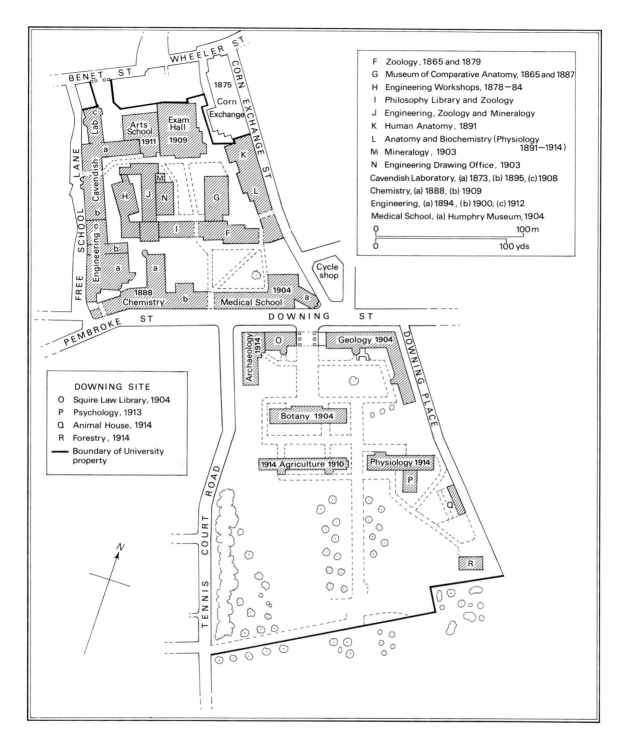

F   Zoology, 1865 and 1879
G   Museum of Comparative Anatomy, 1865 and 1887
H   Engineering Workshops, 1878–84
I   Philosophy Library and Zoology
J   Engineering, Zoology and Mineralogy
K   Human Anatomy, 1891
L   Anatomy and Biochemistry (Physiology 1891–1914)
M   Mineralogy, 1903
N   Engineering Drawing Office, 1903
Cavendish Laboratory, (a) 1873, (b) 1895, (c) 1908
Chemistry, (a) 1888, (b) 1909
Engineering, (a) 1894, (b) 1900, (c) 1912
Medical School, (a) Humphry Museum, 1904

0   100 m
0   100 yds

DOWNING SITE
O   Squire Law Library, 1904
P   Psychology, 1913
Q   Animal House, 1914
R   Forestry, 1914
── Boundary of University
    property

N

Development by 1914

41

with other bodies; money had to be raised before it could be spent. New courses, particularly those in the sciences, meant that there was a need for both new buildings and for new teachers. How these would fit with existing College and University institutions was not always clear, and sometimes they must have seemed a serious threat to the ancient order. But in fact they grew up alongside the existing institutions, sometimes even developing out of them. For all the rhetorical conservatism, Cambridge often managed to do quite startling things.

The changing physical face of Cambridge was perhaps the most dramatic. By the end of the century, the area bounded by Free School Lane, Downing Street, Corn Exchange Street and Wheeler Street had been transformed from a garden and town houses into a 'strong city' for the Museums of Science. In medieval times, this land, at the very heart of the town and just off the market square, had been occupied by an Augustinian priory. The ground had been bought in 1760 by Richard Walker, then the Vice-Master of Trinity and by him given to the University for a Botanic Garden. It served that purpose until 1852, when the plants were moved to the present garden further to the south towards Trumpington. Besides Dr Walker's garden, the area contained a medley of private properties and the University gradually bought these up as occasion offered, achieving ownership of the whole site in 1897. The first University building was erected in 1784 when a piece of land at the south-east corner of the Botanical Garden was considered a 'proper Spot' for the erection of a lecture room and two private rooms for the use of the Professor of Botany and the Jacksonian Professor of Natural Experimental Philosophy, and in 1832–3 followed a building for a Professor of Anatomy, and 'some small accommodation' for the Professors of Chemistry and Physic was added to the older apartments. Apart from some accommodation in the Colleges (the Observatory, for example, was until 1797 on the top of the Great Gate at Trinity, and there was some laboratory space in Downing and St John's Colleges), these were the only buildings specifically devoted to science.[65]

The establishment of the Natural Sciences Tripos in 1848 pointed the need for the provision of museums, laboratories and lecture rooms on a totally different scale to that hitherto attempted; and the removal of the Botanic Garden to its new place suggested a site.

> The usual steps were taken; the usual opposition was offered; much time was wasted in overcoming it; and finally (1863) the central buildings were begun from designs drawn by A. Salvin, architect, but suggested and controlled by Rob. Willis, M.A., Jacksonian Professor. These buildings were intended to accommodate Zoology, Botany, Mineralogy, Mechanism (then dealt with by the Jacksonian Professor); and the Lucasian, Lowndean, and Plumian Professors.[66]

[65] J. W. Clark, *A Concise Guide to the Town and University of Cambridge in Four Walks* (Cambridge, 1898), 131–2.
[66] *Ibid.*, 132.

It was fortunate, J. W. Clark was to write later, apparently without irony, that the buildings, ready for occupation in 1865, were 'constructed of a material and in a style which readily admitted of extension, addition, and alteration'.[67] And indeed it is remarkable that at a time when the only constraints on putting up new University buildings were lack of cash and the prejudices of one's colleagues, the builders were hardly off the site. The introduction of the study of heat, electricity and magnetism into the Mathematical Tripos in the mid-1860s forced the conclusion that the Colleges could not provide adequate instruction in them and that a well-appointed laboratory was indispensable if the study of those subjects was to be taken seriously. The dons dithered about the expense (£6,300 for building and equipping a laboratory; £500 a year for stipends, since the existing Professors in science refused to take on extra work), but the Duke of Devonshire, then Chancellor of the University, helped to push matters forward by writing to the Vice-Chancellor that he was willing to pay for the building and apparatus 'so soon as the University shall have in other respects completed its arrangements for teaching experimental physics and shall have approved the plan of the building'.[68] And so space was found for the Cavendish Laboratory on the New Museums site, and money was squeezed out most ingeniously to meet the conditions of the Chancellor's gift. Gradually, by similar stratagems, other laboratories and class-rooms filled the site – for physiology, anatomy, chemistry and eventually, in 1894, a new engineering laboratory was formed, partly by adapting the old buildings of the Perse Grammar School (bought in 1888), partly by the erection of a new building designed by W. C. Marshall.

Although the University continued to proclaim that it had no money to build, an opportunity arose in 1902 to buy from Downing College, for the huge sum of £25,000, land lying across the street from the New Museums site. This was the 'most central vacant piece of land that is, or is likely to be, in the market'. Even the Registrary, whose uncle, Robert Willis, had overseen the early development of the science buildings, balked at this purchase on the grounds that such expenditure now would 'put out of reach the possibility of undertaking anything else'. But those in favour of further expansion held the day, arguing that given 'the probable needs of the University thirty years hence' they would agree to the purchase even though 'entailing grave inconvenience in the present'.[69] The inconvenience was not long-lived; for even by 1 March 1904 there were buildings on the Downing site fit to be opened by the King himself. Indeed, the progress of science in Cambridge during only fifty years had changed dramatically the visible form of the University and Town.

The significance of this, of course, went beyond mere physical appearances. Cambridge was becoming a major centre of scientific learning and this was indicated

[67] *Ibid.*   [68] Quoted by Winstanley, *Later Victorian Cambridge*, 196.   [69] *CR*, 8 May 1902, 294.

10   The entrance to the Cavendish Laboratory, Free School Lane, 1900.

11   One of the laboratories in the Cavendish, photograph taken in the middle
1890s.

by the large number of honours students who took their degrees from the Natural
Sciences Tripos. But the intellectual change was even more marked. Cambridge
scientists were making discovery after discovery, and some of this was coming into the
popular domain. In November 1905, the Master of Trinity presided in Hall over a
lecture by one of the Fellows, Professor J. J. Thomson, who 'described to a large audience some of his recent experiments and mathematical investigations which have led to
such a notable change in our ideas of the structure of matter'. Thomson referred to the
thought of ancient Greece, but he showed how his new theories about the complex
structure of the atom were derived from simple and repeatable experimental data.[70]

[70] *Ibid.*, 30 November 1905, 120.

12   The Vice-Chancellor (Dr Frederick Henry Chase, President of Queens' College) and the University Registrary (John Willis Clark) accompany their Majesties the King and Queen in procession to the Senate-House, 1 March 1904, on the occasion of the opening of new buildings for law, medicine, geology and botany.

What is new is exciting; but it can also unsettle as well; and was there a danger that the scientists, despite being well grounded in Latin and Greek, were taking over the University? Already people were adjusting to this potentially grim thought by making light of it: there was but one great University in the country, someone said: Oxford, 'with a scientific suburb, specifically designated Cambridge'.[71] And so there was particular felicity in the thought of the young classical scholar, living in Trinity alongside the greatest scientific minds of the time, that, in general, scientists might be

71 *Ibid.*, 19 October 1905, 5.

13 The Botanical School, Downing Site, 1904, architect W. C. Marshall, opened by HM King Edward VII on 1 March. The new building contained lecture rooms, laboratories, a museum and a herbarium 'the storehouse of collections given to the University by successive occupants of the Chair of Botany, since its foundation in 1724, and by various travellers, among whom the honoured name of Charles Darwin is conspicuous' (*Reporter 1903–4*, 563). It cost upwards of £25,000 (£1.4 million at 1992 prices) to build and fit out, almost all of which had come from the successful appeal organised by the Chancellor from 1899 onwards.

like those 'men that were in cumbrance and in debt and troubled in their hearts' who gathered unto David at Adullam;[72] even if they were, in their rough way, also like David, poised at their 'series of caves near Downing Street' to capture the Kingdom.

[72] 1 Samuel 22:1. William Tyndale's translation. In 1866 'Adullamite' was used famously by John Bright as a nickname for a group of Liberal Members of Parliament, led by R. Lowe and E. Horsman, who seceded from the Liberal Party out of dissatisfaction with Lord John Russell's attempt to carry a measure of Parliamentary reform.

The very success of the scientists to stake out territory and to build on it, threw into stark contrast the failure to grapple with the problems of the University Library. The main requirement was for more space for books; but the Library occupied a much more sensitive site than the science buildings: namely, rooms in the Old Schools at the end of King's Parade and next to the Senate-House, the very heart of the ancient University. Any proposal to improve or expand the accommodation was bound to be the subject of intense scrutiny and to provide the occasion for emotional debate: for what, in a University, arouses more passion than books and librarians? Basil Champneys, who had erected distinguished buildings for Newnham College, was consulted by the Library Syndicate as far back as the late 1870s for ideas as to how more room could be found for the Library on its existing site. In May 1879, the Syndicate brought forward Champneys' imaginative suggestion that the eastern quadrangle of the Old Schools be roofed over with a structure of iron and glass, and the resulting covered space filled with book-shelves and reading desks. But the scheme did not find favour and was dropped.

By the end of the century, however, the limits of making do had been reached and the Syndicate presented a major report to the University on the organisation of the Library.[73] They pointed out the need for more, and more specialist, staff (the establishment then consisted of a total of nineteen people from the Librarian down to the domestic servants), for a re-arrangement of books in the existing rooms (itself not an uncontroversial matter, at least so far as it concerned the placing of the books on law), and for new building. Some relief on the first two heads, together with agreement that the annual sum allowed for the maintenance of the Library be increased from £5,000 to £5,500, was eventually gained; but any scheme for new building was beyond the wit of man to get through the Senate.

The Syndicate's main proposal was to resurrect Champneys' design of roofing the eastern quadrangle. Not only would this provide space for 20,000 books at ground-floor level alone, but further minor building work, including enclosing the colonnade on the east front of the building to give better access to the ground floor of the Library and to increase supervision and security, together with a more radical re-allocation of accommodation in the Old Schools, would add more book-stacks and seats for readers. The Report met with mixed reception, but, on condition that nothing was done without further vote of the Senate, the Library Syndicate were allowed to consult Mr Marshall to bring Champneys' scheme up to date. By May 1900, the Syndicate, now under the chairmanship of Henry Jackson as the Vice-Chancellor's deputy, were ready to report again. There was vigorous discussion, and the Syndicate thought it prudent to bring an amended scheme before the Senate in November of the

---

[73] *Reporter* 1898–9, 197–203.

same year. Despite opposition, they seemed to gain some ground, for on 31 January 1901 Graces were approved allowing the Syndicate to obtain tenders for the work before reporting again to the University.[74]

The costs turned out to be relatively modest – all could be done, including the fitting out, for £6,463 19s 9d. But at the Discussion on 25 May 1901 it became clear that the Syndicate had no chance of getting the proposals through as they stood. So during the summer they modified their plans and came back with a scheme, not much less expensive, but shorn of the proposal to enclose the colonnade and to mess with the arrangements for the law books. The amended Report was discussed on 5 November. Opening the proceedings, the Vice-Chancellor announced that the Financial Board had had an opportunity to scrutinise the costings and, finding that, among other things, the Library Syndicate had omitted to make provision for a clerk of works, had minuted that the University be asked to allocate £7,000 for the alterations to the building.[75]

But the opposition had the bit between its teeth. The scientists, sensing an opportunity for making trouble among their more refined colleagues, let it be known even before the Discussion took place that they were against the scheme partly because, in their view, it only tinkered with the problem: at least £500,000 would need to be expended to make the Library really useful, therefore the University should not be content to go for half-measures now, thus delaying a more satisfactory long-term outcome. And, they added mischievously, many of the present difficulties experienced by the Library lay at the feet of the Copyright Act, obliging the University to house 'miles of inferior novels, inferior music, inferior periodicals',[76] which were of no use to serious students. At the Discussion itself the attack focussed on the shortcomings of the proposed alterations to the buildings. Parts of the Library would be dark and unventilated: it was not good enough for members of the Senate to have to be sent down into the stacks 'with a lantern as into a well, and if the light did not go out with the foul air, it would be alright'.[77] An electric fan, installed to move the air, would be noisy and disturb readers, notoriously tetchy characters at the best of times (they would later petition the Provost and Fellows of King's College with the suggestion that their raucous peacock 'would form a graceful item on the menu' for luncheon when the King came to Cambridge).[78] Was there really need to find so much new space when the maps and geography books could surely be moved to the geological museum 'now rearing its somewhat ungainly form' on the Downing site, and the problems of

---

[74] *Ibid.*, *1899–1900*, 892, 1015; *ibid.*, *1900–1*, 197–9, 519.
[75] *Ibid.*, *1900–1*, 895, 947–56; *ibid.*, *1901–2*, 89, 180–7.
[76] *CR*, 31 October 1901, 34.
[77] *Reporter 1901–2*, 184.
[78] *CR*, 25 February 1904, 212.

14 Interior of the University Library at the turn of the nineteenth and
twentieth centuries.

Law would in due course be solved with the erection of the proposed Squire Law Library, also in Downing Street.[79]

Professor Ridgeway was scathing of the Syndicate's claim to virtue for having listened to the Senate in the summer and withdrawing gracefully their plan to fill in the arches of the colonnade: this part of the scheme, he alleged, had not been dropped gracefully but with a sullen temper. Working himself into a frenzy, he argued that

> If the Senate was so weak as to be wheedled into roofing over the Eastern Quadrangle, plunging [the rooms] into Cimmerian darkness ... his own impression was that, having voted a large amount of money for electric fans and horse power, the next thing the Senate would be asked to do would be to knock down the eastern wall of the Law Room and close the facade ... In having saved the facade at the present moment, let not members of the Senate think that they had saved it for ever.

And he concluded that the old quadrangle had been an essential part of University life for 500 years: 'Did they want to throw away their past and to level themselves down to an American university or to a provincial university which had no past to live by?'[80] As the *Cambridge Review* commented, while Professor Ridgeway's speech 'was not altogether convincing, at least [it] left the impression that there were no other possible defects in the scheme, however infinitesimal, that could be brought to light'.[81] Not surprisingly, when the Grace to implement the scheme was put to the Senate, it was lost, on a very high turnout, by 177 votes to 158. Another generation was to pass before the Library got its new building.[82]

Perhaps it was that the development of the New Museums site had convinced 'everybody but the pure utilitarians among us' of 'the danger of any architectural change whatsoever. Till it is possible to build a museum that is not either an attempt to emulate a government barracks, or to copy the section of a piece of bacon, many will hesitate to sanction any change to buildings, which if not masterpieces, are worthy of

[79] *Reporter 1901–2*, 185.   [80] *Ibid*.   [81] *CR*, 7 November 1901, 50.

[82] *Reporter 1901–2*, 259. The University Library holds a copy of *Microcosmographia Academica* (Adv.e.119.1.) given by A. F. Schofield (Librarian 1923–49) to his predecessor, Henry Jenkinson, in which he has annotated the line about meeting casually of an afternoon in King's Parade, 'particularly that part of it which lies between the Colleges of Pembroke and Caius' in order to fix things up by adding that Leonard Whibley was a Fellow of Pembroke and Sir W. Ridgeway a Fellow of Caius. Both men were regular scourges of the Librarian, particularly when it came to the question of a new building and the arrangement of the books. The University Library eventually found new quarters on open space (belonging to King's and Clare) in west Cambridge. The move was seen through by the determination of, among others, Sir Hugh Anderson, Master of Caius. The very radical proposal to move the Library on to a new site was discussed by the Senate on 24 February 1921. Ridgeway gave a classic performance, but Christopher Brooke writes that on this occasion his 'speech was so comparatively urbane as to make me suspect that he and Anderson had been in conclave'. Brooke, *History of the University*, 375.

the University which they adorn.'[83] But, while scientists were men of the world, willing to follow a leader who was able to grab all the money that was going, those who used the University Library were more individual and idiosyncratic in their view of the University world; and, if truth be told, they were much more opinionated about how the Library should be run. Consequently, because they could not agree among themselves what it was precisely that they wanted, they could not form a large enough party to get it; and because they were so fearful of change, they got nothing, and were left to brood in their cramped and difficult quarters instead.

The Statutory Commissions of 1881–2 may not have done to the Colleges and the University all that some radicals would have wished; but they did lay down the ground-rules for levying a tax on the Colleges to pay for University purposes. This made possible some of the new developments and allowed some flexibility in the creation of new posts. The Colleges grumbled at the wickedness of it all, but then, as more recently, some of them voluntarily offered more (provided of course that the University accepted the benefaction for the purposes the College concerned wished to support: Trinity financed several initiatives, the most notable being support for Michael Foster in a new post in physiology). But the Colleges were still too poor and too deeply tied to existing commitments for them to be able to give the University all the money it needed: after all, even Lautenschlager's Bacteria-crushing machines, which no Pathological Laboratory could do without, cost £45 each.[84] So a determined effort was made at the turn of the century to 're-endow' Cambridge.

A detailed analysis of the University's financial affairs appeared in the *Times* in April 1897 and this was followed by the suggestion from William Chawner, the Master of Emmanuel, among others, that perhaps the time had come for a general appeal to be put out. The Master of Emmanuel preferred to put his trust in many small subscriptions from alumni, rather than hope of big bequests from millionaires. Not everyone was happy, since the whole idea of an appeal evoked in 'many minds a feeling of humiliation, that a great University should feel it incumbent upon her to take the position of begging for guineas.' And others thought that the trouble lay in 'trying to do too much at once and to the over-rapid development of scientific and medical departments'.[85] Mr R. F. Scott pointed the

> oft-repeated moral about the comparative cheapness of a classical or mathematical training, and deprecated the introduction of the engineering department. It is indeed a true saying that democratic schemes are always the most costly. And there can be no doubt that if the dream of some enthusiasts be ever realised and a real training in Natural

[83] *CR*, 5 June 1901, 354.
[84] This machine, bought at the request of the Professors of Physiology, Botany and Pathology, 'supplies a much felt want.' *Reporter 1898–9*, 204. Michael Young tried hard without success to find out from his colleagues what the machine actually did.
[85] *CR*, 21 October 1897, 18; 28 October 1897, 34; 4 November 1897, 50.

Science becomes as universal as a Classical education was once, the country will find its education bill costs three times what it used to do.[86]

Mr Chawner, in an interview with the *Daily Mail*, agreed that the 'poverty' of the University was due not to 'the older studies, but solely to the medical and scientific development of the University,' and he 'expressed himself as strongly opposed either to a Government grant or to a further attack on the incomes of the Colleges'. For this, the editors of the *Cambridge Review* noted that 'indeed ... we are thankful for small mercies'.[87]

Nevertheless, a University Benefaction Fund was started, and by January of 1899 some £10,000 had been raised. Significantly, about half came from the dons themselves, £1,000 being contributed by the Hon. Bertrand Russell alone.[88] There was a need, however, for a more co-ordinated approach; and with characteristic wariness the Chancellor called a meeting of eminent persons to his house in London on 31 January 1899 to launch the Cambridge University Association.[89] He referred to the earlier publicity and the surrounding controversy; but his analysis of the way forward was very clear: the University and the Colleges had endowments, but they tended to be endowments in land or in securities connected with land. Over recent years, agricultural incomes had diminished. The Colleges were hard pressed to maintain themselves and to carry out existing educational work; and they had proved utterly unable to provide increased financial support for the University on the scale which had been envisaged by the Statutory Commission of 1877.

While fairly equipped for the older branches of knowledge, the Colleges could not be expected to provide for newer branches, nor for advanced study, nor for research. Moreover, 'If they did attempt to make such a provision it would be a wasteful attempt, and it is to the University, and the University alone, as distinguished from the Colleges of Cambridge, that we must look for expansion and effort in this direction.' University income (by 1910 about £60,000 a year of which £18,000 came from College contributions) had not increased in proportion to the expansion of its duties and its work. Some heads of income were stationary, or even diminishing, and student fees had been raised to the limit of productiveness. It seemed, if you did a hard calculation, that the increased number of students who availed themselves of University (as opposed to College) teaching, actually cost the University more than they contributed to its revenues. The University was deficient in buildings and 'crippled in the provision of the necessary educational staff'. Out of twenty readerships 'contemplated,

---

[86] *Ibid.*, 4 November 1897, 50.   [87] *Ibid.*   [88] *Ibid.*, 16 June 1898, 403.

[89] The Vice-Chancellor had mentioned in his address to the Senate on 1 October 1898 that at the desire of the Chancellor a 'very influential committee of University men' had been formed to see how best to raise money to put up new buildings on 'the admirable and central sites' recently purchased by the University and to deal with the problem of overcrowding and inadequate housing faced by 'many departments of the University'. *Reporter 1898–9*, 9. But the Cambridge University Association was not formally launched until the following year.

and I believe actually directed to be founded by the statutes of 1882, it has only been possible to found eight', and these at lower stipends than was hoped for. Aid must come to Cambridge, either from the State or from private munificence. Leaving aside the question as to whether Parliament would actually be prepared to vote public money, subvention from the Government was not really acceptable as a solution to the problem without considering 'what risk of interference with its independence, and the general character of its teaching, may be apprehended by the acceptance of such aid'. No, the answer lay in private benefaction, an appeal to the University's cosmopolitan alumni. The Chancellor concluded by estimating the current need: £200,000 for new buildings and an endowment of £300,000 to provide an annual income of £2,000 for maintenance and £10,000 a year for new teaching posts. This target of £500,000 was equivalent to £26 million in 1990s money.[90]

The Vice-Chancellor followed the Duke of Devonshire by stressing that existing endowments even failed to meet the current demands

> not only of what your Grace has called the new sciences – the new subjects – but also of the old. It is true that the student of natural science requires laboratories and museums: but it is also true that the classic, wandering beyond the mere writings of the ancients and wishing to study their art and archaeology and antiquities, requires now-a-days appliances more costly than a classical dictionary and the works of a few Greek and Latin authors.

There was a natural expansion of knowledge and this implied and demanded a 'multiplication of teaching-appliances and the subdivision of subjects of research'.[91] Professor George Darwin, the Plumian Professor of Astronomy and Experimental Philosophy, reminded the distinguished gathering, in a way that would not seem out of place a century later, that Cambridge led science in the country, for, taking the 3,021 pages dealing with physical and mathematical subjects published in the *Philosophical Transactions of the Royal Society* for the three years 1896–8, some 1,624 had been written by Cambridge men, and no less than 915 of those pages by scientists actually resident in the University. The statistic was not quite so favourable for the biological sciences, for there Cambridge men had written but 794 of the 2,459 pages of the *Transactions* devoted to biology, though of those pages 409 had been contributed by Cambridge residents. Besides, there was here a special case, for the leading journal in physiology was published not by the Royal Society but by Cambridge itself, and the University produced a good journal in anatomy also. Taken all in all, the conclusion was that 'nearly one half of British science emanates from our University', and this certainly justified the expenditure on it.[92]

90 *CR*, Special Supplement 16 February 1899: 'Cambridge University Association Report of the Meeting held at Devonshire House, on Tuesday, January 31st, 1899, to Inaugurate the Association', iii–v.
91 *Ibid.*, v.   92 *Ibid.*, x.

The Registrary, while not overlooking the need for new science buildings, felt constrained to point out that priority must be 'additional accommodation at the Library, which is, of course, the fountain head of all knowledge in the place', and he put in a plea for new business premises – 'we practically have none at present'. Before the meeting dispersed, the Chancellor had put £10,000 to the re-endowment of the University, Lord Rothschild had indicated that his bank would contribute a similar sum and the Drapers Company indicated that they would pay for a Professor of Agriculture.[93]

The appeal was relatively successful: at the Chancellor's death in 1908, the Association had raised £115,000 (approximately £5.5 million in 1992 values) for the University. Science and buildings had benefited enormously, but they were not the only outcome of the successful appeal. Substantial contributions had made possible the Quick Professorship of Biology; the Brereton and Jebb funds had been set up for Classics; the City of London Livery Companies gave for the University Library, for Russian and for Forestry; the citizens of Huddersfield were collecting for a lectureship in Pathology; and Miss Squire had given to the Faculty of Law.[94] Among the donations from humbler individuals, it was noticeable that there was much ear-marking for law and medicine. But these were areas where the appetite was never satisfied. Medicine in particular had constant need – of beds (which involved delicate negotiation between the Regius Professor of Physic and the Governors of Dr Addenbrooke's Hospital) and bodies. Lugubriously, Cornford sang[95]

A Ballad of Cadavers:
Or, the MATERIAL Needs of the Medical School

Eighteen men on a dead man's chest!
    Ho, ho, ho! and isn't it rum?
Eight and a half get through at the best,
Want of Cadavers has done for the rest;
    Ho, for a miserly dividen*dum!* – *Old Song.*

When students to Cadavers are
    As eighteen is to one,
The dividend's inadequate,
    The thing cannot be done!

When *two* must share an arm or leg,
    And *four* take heart and neck,
Some forty-three per cent may pass –
    The rest will be a 'wreck'.

[93] *Ibid.*, xi.   [94] *Ibid.*, 30 April 1908, 321.   [95] *Ibid.*, 29 January 1903, 149.

At Owens' and at Birmingham
  'One man, one leg,' 's the rule:
And students have a head a-piece
  At happy Liverpool.

One guinea there for *three whole parts*
  As winter price they fix:
Two more in summer may be had
  Dirt cheap – for twelve-and-six!

At Edinburgh (strange, but true!)
  One 'subject' does for *twenty*!
But when the Professor's 'satisfied,'
  You get *half* – parts in plenty.

But London's best: there, eight to one's
  The odds, of men to parts:
When I am a cadaver,
  I mean to go to Bart's.

Dissatisfaction with the material resources for study was not the only thing to stir the dons. Few matters raised so loud a cry as attempts to reform the Tripos, especially that in the older subjects of mathematics and classics. In these subjects everyone had an expert opinion, and every proposal for change was the object of impassioned scrutiny. Moreover, those primarily responsible for teaching the subject had not only to agree among themselves about what changes were desirable, but they then had to persuade the Senate as a whole that changes should be made. In the case of mathematics, there was near unanimity about what needed to be done, but the mathematicians were thwarted by the Senate at large; in the case of classics, the classicists themselves were divided, making the progress of reform through the Senate well-nigh impossible.

The Mathematical Tripos had been the subject of extensive reform in 1882, and the regulations under which it was conducted had been largely unchanged since coming fully into force in 1886. The Tripos was normally taken by students in June at the end of their third year of residence, and this was sufficient to obtain the BA degree. A more specialised examination was offered for advanced students the following year. But since the 1880s, while the total number of students at Cambridge had been increasing, the number studying mathematics was in sharp decline. Partly this was ascribed to the attractiveness of the new courses in physics and engineering; partly to the technical nature of the papers, though it was also admitted that candidates tended to ignore the difficult questions and, in their quest for marks, concentrated on writing elegant though conventional answers to as many questions as possible; partly the Tripos was unpopular because it was difficult for men of moderate capacity to perform reasonably well in an examination which published its results in a single order of merit; and partly, as the century drew to a close, fewer students saw mathematics as a good subject for general education.

The answer seemed to be to have a scheme of examinations in which a Part I was taken at the end of the second year of study. This would be taught from books and would aim to provide a basic grounding in the subject. There would be class divisions, but no order of merit. The examination in itself would not qualify students for a degree, enabling those who wished to change course and go on to study law, history, physics, engineering, moral sciences etc. Others could finish their degree with a further examination in mathematics, which would be more challenging, would include a wide range of subjects not too rigidly defined and would be less susceptible to cramming. For this examination an order of merit might be retained. Really advanced work in the subject, however, should not be tested by examination, but left to graduate work and be rewarded by competitive scholarships and fellowships.[96]

By the Lent term of 1900, matters were ready to be put to the vote. Few people other than the mathematicians themselves pretended to understand the more complex technical aspects of the proposed reforms, but everyone understood that the scheme meant the death of the order of merit in the Tripos, and hence the prestigious position of the Senior Wrangler (the top student in the year). Thus the arguments were emotive ones, barely touching on the merits of the scheme, and the reform was lost, on a very rainy day, by 161 votes to 129. All the leading mathematicians and scientists had campaigned for a placet vote. But they had not been successful. As the *Cambridge Review* put it, 'The result is disheartening for the advocates of the change. Why the voting should be on one side and the weight of specially qualified opinion on the other would be a matter for curious inquiry. It is not the first time that this has been so in recent years. Perhaps our constitution – but no, perish the thought!'[97] Eventually, reform was achieved in 1906.

The fate of classics is particularly instructive. Cornford's mentor, Henry Jackson, was a prominent reformer in later nineteenth-century Cambridge. Moreover, he was 'politically wise as well as enlightened, and therefore not likely to indulge in extravagances'.[98] He did much to promote the welfare and efficiency of his College and he led the campaigns to breathe life into the teaching of classics. After many years of delay and deliberation, the University finally agreed in the summer of 1879 to a new structure for the Classical Tripos. With effect from examinations to be held for the first time in 1881 and 1882, the Tripos was to be divided into two parts: the first would continue to be a test of what was described as 'pure scholarship', that is, knowledge of language examined by translation and composition, and success in this examination

96 *Ibid.*, 25 February 1897, 254–5.   97 *Ibid.*, 22 February 1900, 216.
98 Winstanley, *Later Victorian Cambridge*, 237.

15 Henry Jackson, OM LittD (1839–1921), by William Rothenstein. Jackson was the eldest son of an eminent Sheffield surgeon. He went up to Trinity in 1858, became a Fellow in 1864 and Vice-Master in 1914. In 1906 he succeeded Sir Richard Jebb as Regius Professor of Greek and was appointed to the Order of Merit in 1908. He was an ardent reformer throughout his life – his last appearance in public was when he was carried to the Senate-House in 1921 to vote again in favour of degrees for women. The drawing dates from 1904.

alone qualified students for an honours degree; but the second part, besides imposing a further compulsory test of linguistic skills, introduced sections in ancient philosophy, ancient history, archaeology and language, designed to broaden the scope of classical learning and to encourage both specialist knowledge of particular subjects and a better understanding of the civilisation of the ancient world.

A debate about the balance between 'pure scholarship' and knowledge of the subject matter of the authors read had been going on for over twenty years. Jackson, who had served as secretary to the Board of Classics which had worked out the new scheme, justified the development by attacking the Tripos he himself had taken where students

> read Thucydides, but not Grote; they studied the construction of the speeches, but did not confuse themselves by trying to study their drift. They read the *Phaedrus*, but had no Theory of Ideas. They read the *Theaetetus*, but did not know what Plato was driving at or what Protagoras meant. They read twenty or thirty letters of Cicero – they took care to read selected letters – but they did not look into a Roman history in connection with them.[99]

But the defenders of the *status quo* maintained that, while the proposed scheme made generous provision for students with special knowledge of the optional subjects ('in any of which', a critic of the reform observed, 'it would be possible to take a high place with but little classical knowledge'[100], it ignored the needs of those who were widely read in classical literature but had not wanted to devote themselves to any particular subject. As such it 'seems difficult to imagine how a more fatal blow could be given to a study of classics as a liberal and valuable means of education than by the proposed scheme ... which not merely sets a premium on special reading, but absolutely affords men of high *general* attainments in classics no opportunity to distinguish themselves'.[101] The reform of 1879, however, by recommending the division of the Tripos into two completely separate parts, effected a reconciliation between opposing demands. It was marked by both pragmatism and compromise, ensuring not only that it would secure the necessary support for its approval but that the underlying debate would be continued.

During Cornford's entire undergraduate years the classicists disputed with each other about the Tripos. For some years there had been 'a widespread feeling of dissatisfaction with regard to the working of the Classical Tripos' and so in December 1896 the Special Board for Classics set up a committee to consider schemes for reform. They consulted widely, sending out questionnaires to lecturers and examiners and writing letters to non-resident scholars and masters in the chief public schools. The replies showed unequivocally that

[99] *Ibid.*, 211.   [100] T. E. Page, quoted *ibid.*, 221.   [101] *Ibid.*

the need for change was great and urgent: that the present system, by which so large a majority of candidates take their degree on Part I alone, did not ensure an education of adequate breadth. The merits of Part I as a training and an examination in Scholarship were generally admitted, but its inadequacy as the sole test of Classical study was strongly emphasised.[102]

The Special Board, now under Jackson's chairmanship, decided to put this right. They proposed that no one should be able to take an honours degree on the strength of Part I alone; that the existing Part II, which had introduced a strong element of disciplinary specialisation (and which had not been very successful in attracting students, other than those who wished to be dons), should become a new Part III, and that a new examination 'of a more general character (to be called Part II) should be instituted, in which the different sides of classical life and thought should be studied in connexion with the original authors'. The Report, agreed in the Easter term of 1898 by sixteen out of the twenty-five members of the Board, was published in the *Reporter* on 11 October and discussed over two sessions on 3 and 11 November.[103]

Hardly anyone said that nothing should be done; but many were dissatisfied with the new proposals, either in general or in detail. The main critics saw a sinister move behind the measures to devalue knowledge of the ablative absolute in the face of fashionable new interests in history, archaeology, philosophy and religion. Some thought that the old Part I was a perfectly respectable course, 'educationally at least quite as good as the training given by the Natural Science Tripos, Part I, or perhaps by the Mathematical Tripos, Part I', and in an apparent desire to increase the scope of classics and to raise the standards, it was wrong not to leave in place an examination whose academic level might be regarded as 'ample for the weaker men'.[104] The more general course to be offered in the new Part II was at once too demanding and too superficial. No one could possibly read all that was to be required, nor attend the lectures. Moreover, there was a sneaking suspicion that it was being put in to help candidates in the civil service examinations grub up a few more facts to get more marks. But if that were so 'They might turn out journalists perhaps, they might turn out Indian civil servants, they would likely turn out a set of conceited prigs, but they would certainly not turn out educated men.'[105] A much more modest tinkering would do. The Master of Christ's, regretting, as an old reformer, that he was now 'parted off from men of his own standing, with whom in the past he had been agreed', regretting even more 'to differ from younger classical teachers, for whose ability he had an unfeigned respect', admitted to the Senate that although he had no longer the advantage of youth, he

[102] *Reporter* 1898–9, 45.   [103] *Ibid.*, 45–51, 239–46, 284–98.   [104] The Master of Christ's. *Ibid.*, 285.
[105] R. D. Archer-Hind, *ibid.*, 290. The large classics staff at Trinity were thus divided on the merits of reform.

did not look upon himself exactly as obstructive, and he had certainly helped to change this Tripos more than once. But he confessed that he had learnt one thing, that every great change produced some of the good they expected, and also a considerable amount of evil which they did not expect, and in that conviction he pleaded that the change, if change there should be, might be as small as possible.[106]

In the face of this onslaught, the Classics Board published a revised Report in February 1899. They dropped altogether their proposals for a new Part II, but amended those for the old Part II to add to it a general section alongside the more specialist sections, which would contain study of a short set period and an outline paper on Greek and Roman history. The critics were not satisfied. In a series of Graces, they approved without difficulty the affirmation of the Tripos as consisting of two Parts. That Part I alone should cease to qualify a student for a degree was defeated by 119 votes to 89, and that it should be taken not later than the end of the second year of residence (to allow more time for specialist study) was also defeated by 123 votes to 64. The inclusion of a new general section in Part II was lost by 103 to 51; and several other proposals of detail were either non-placeted without a count, or were withdrawn.[107] So very little had been gained, except an airing of opinions and just 'one more illustration at once of the highly conservative character of the University at present, and of the extreme difficulty of securing a majority in favour of any proposal on which the experts are much divided'.[108] In calmer mood the following year, however, the Classics Board got through (though not without continued opposition) a proposal that two new papers, covering 'Literature, Philosophy, and Archaeology (limited to Sculpture and Architecture)' be included to toughen up Part I, but only on condition that candidates would not have to study more than two of the three subjects proposed.[109]

It was perhaps, then, rash of Francis Cornford in 1903 to address the newly formed Cambridge Classical Society (whose constitution expressly included the ladies of Girton and Newnham in its membership[110]) on the subject of 'The Cambridge Classical Course: An Essay in Anticipation of Further Reform.' He prefaced his remarks with the anecdote 'Lord Rea said to Sir David Ramsay, "Well, God mend all!" Ramsay answered, "Nay, by God, Donald, we must help Him to mend it."'[111] Cornford's plea was for change now, because he foresaw an 'organised assault' being made upon 'what is called Classical Education'. The subject was under threat, not just in the Universities, but in the schools and in the minds of all literate people. Not only the present

---

[106] *Ibid.*, 286.   [107] *Ibid.*, 555–62, 673–5.   [108] *CR*, 16 March 1899, 270.
[109] *Reporter 1899–1900*, 763–5, 906–13, 1052.
[110] The Society had been founded on the initiative of Sir Richard Jebb, Regius Professor of Greek, Fellow of Trinity and for some time one of the University's representatives in the House of Commons, at a meeting held in Peterhouse on 9 May 1903; Francis Cornford was the first Secretary of the Society, and at a meeting held on 15 June a provisional constitution was agreed, including the proposal that the Society include 'past and present members of the staffs of Girton College and Newnham College'. *CR*, 30 April 1903, 258; 17 June 1903, 374.
[111] F. M. Cornford, *The Cambridge Classical Course: An Essay in Anticipation of Further Reform*, (Cambridge, 1903), 5.

predominance of classics would be challenged, 'but its right to bare existence.'[112] And in order to avoid this impending disaster, it was no good to embark on an

> obstinate and blind defence of our system as it exists at present but by a frank avowal of its defects and a declaration, to which at the same time our actions must testify, that we are willing to remedy them. To valid criticism the proper answer is reform. When the criticism, whether friendly or hostile, gives warning of a determined and powerful onset, it is merely prudent that the reform should begin without delay.[113]

Cornford then went on to set out the case for the rescue of classics. Much that was in the present syllabus, whether at school or University, was redundant or defective. Of course everyone must have a thorough grasp of syntax, moods and tenses,

> but let us recognise that a thorough grasp of ideas is a thing of worth, and quite distinct from a superficial 'viewiness'. To retain the full bulk of the old linguistic examination is precisely to encourage a hasty treatment of the new subjects. If these last are to be of real value for education, room must be cleared, and time allowed, for thoroughness in this department also.[114]

The defects of the Cambridge course were clear: a place had been found for sculpture and architecture, but not 'for vase-painting, or for coins, or for gems — all of them manageable and fascinating objects of study'. Nothing was being done for mythology and religion 'subjects which may be illustrated from every page of ancient literature'.[115] What was needed was the removal from the formal examinations of all those papers for translation, and the aesthetically worthless papers in prose and verse composition, for which so many students were crammed for so much of their working day. Instead they should be reading widely across the whole range of classical literature, and encouraged to make a real translation — that of the essence of the ideas originally attempted to be conveyed, rather than some literal and mechanical effort that very often made no sense:

> The truth is that command over a foreign language which you cannot talk is gained chiefly by wide and careful reading. A man cannot write it until he has begun to be able to think in it; and he ought not to try. Our most backward students produce week after week pages of stuff, of which you can hardly say more than that the words are Greek or Latin words. We stare impotently at the versions. Not a sentence, not a phrase, is Greek or Latin; and you can no more explain why they are not than you can explain to a deaf man why a casual series of notes is not music.[116]

On the other hand, the very best students already knew all the syntax they needed to know, but were compelled by the exigencies of the examination to waste hours on mindless verse composition and boring translation: they were not encouraged to find

---

[112] *Ibid.*, 5. [113] *Ibid.*, 6. [114] *Ibid.*, 8. [115] *Ibid.* [116] *Ibid.*, 11.

out what the ancient world was actually all about, nor stimulated to embark on a wide ranging enquiry for the truth. And, after all, *L'essential, en effet, dans l'éducation, ce n'est pas la doctrine enseignée, c'est l'éveil.*[117]

But if the subject could not be rescued immediately by reform of the Tripos, then much could be done in practice to minimise the pernicious effects of the formal examination. A more rational organisation of lectures, involving close co-operation between all the Colleges, to cut out needless duplication on bread-and-butter subjects, would allow time for teachers to write new books and to prepare new lectures so as to bring to their students the fruits of new research. For

> the ancient classics resemble the universe. They are always there, and they are very much the same as ever. But as the philosophy of every new age puts a fresh and original construction on the universe, so in the classics scholarship finds a perennial object for ever fresh and original interpretation. A text may be brought so near perfection that further emendation is nearly useless; and then that chapter of our task is closed. But where the editor ends, the work of the interpreter begins. He who supposes that scholarship has no further interest must either know little of Hellenic art and culture, or care little for the knowledge, the appreciation, and the love, of beauty.[118]

It followed that it was no part of a humane education to 'cram' youthful minds or to protect them from books by making them dull and storing them 'in such a way that no one can find them without several years' training'.[119] Perhaps it is in the spirit of Cornford's radicalism about his much-loved subject that our modern Faculty of Classics not only teaches students Greek and Latin from scratch, but elucidates the reign of the Emperor Augustus by reference to the tabloid tribulations of the House of Windsor.[120]

Cornford's fears for the future of classics were not ill-founded. Concurrent with the establishment of the Classical Association, and with Cornford's well-argued plea for sensible reform in the subject, an attack was being mounted on the general importance of classics in University education. When it came, it came from the highest authority in the University: the Chancellor, visiting Cambridge in 1903 to confer honorary

---

[117] Ernest Renan, *Souvenirs d'enfance et de la Jeunesse* (Paris, 1883), 184, quoted *ibid.*, 20. Michael Tilby kindly tracked the quotation to its source for me.

[118] *Ibid.*, 19–20.   [119] *Microcosmographia Academica*, 2nd edition, 22–3. Schofield also sidelined this passage.

[120] Candidates for Part II of the Classics Tripos 1993 offering paper C 2 *The Roman Emperor: Construction and Deconstruction of an Image* were asked 'How far can an analysis of the image of the modern British monarchy help our understanding of the image of the Roman emperor?' and were told that they might wish to refer, in their answer, to a passage from a transcript of an alleged conversation between HRH the Prince of Wales and Mrs Andrew Parker Bowles, and an extract from J. Williamson's 'Royalty and Representation'. The question was replaced in a paper on the same subject in Part II of the Historical Tripos by one thought by the historians to be less 'a-historical' in form.

degrees, took the opportunity to talk informally to the gathered Heads of Houses and Professors at a party held in the Combination Room at Trinity. His drift was that, 'after talking with many men in all parts of England he found an opinion existing that at Cambridge they were devoted to bygone ideals, and that they would not budge one atom to meet the educational ideas of the day.'[121] To the outside world, Cambridge seemed very slow in its espousal of new subjects for study and very out of step with the rest of the British educational system in its requirement for knowledge of two classical languages before students could qualify as candidates for degree examinations. This, the Chancellor considered, was damaging to his appeal for the re-endowment of the University, and it was both politically unwise and socially undesirable. He followed up his meeting with a letter to the Vice-Chancellor, for disclosure to the Council only. As a result, the Council published a Report on 2 November 1903, stating simply that the Vice-Chancellor had had a letter from the Chancellor 'calling attention to certain questions concerning the University and its studies, amongst others the expediency of modifying its requirements with respect to the Classical languages and of enlarging the range of modern subjects.' The Report went on to say that 'It has frequently been urged that changes are desirable in the system of the University, and the need for such changes appears to many to have been increased by the reorganisation of secondary education throughout the country and by recent developments in other Universities.' The Council proposed, therefore, the establishment of a Syndicate 'to consider what changes, if any, are desirable in the studies, teaching, and examinations of the University', which it hoped would be able to report by the end of the Easter term 1904.[122]

The suggestion was controversial. The Grace proposing the establishment of the Syndicate was opposed, but carried by 170 votes to 79. A second Grace determining the membership of the Syndicate was also opposed, but carried by 156 votes to 92.[123] The Syndicate met and consulted widely, but they needed more time for their work. They were not ready to publish their first report until the autumn of 1904. Although they had resolved to focus only on the regulations for the Previous Examination (the examination which students had to pass after coming into residence if they had not already satisfied the academic requirements for being allowed to sit for degree examinations) their proposals were quite revolutionary. The Syndicate stressed that the purpose of the Previous Examination must be to 'guarantee that a student has attained a sound elementary knowledge of the subjects which should form part of a liberal education, and which provide the mental training necessary before any course of special study is undertaken'. It was not possible to impose an examination in all such subjects,

---

121 The Master of Christ's version of what the Chancellor had said. *Reporter 1904–5*, 387.
122 *Ibid.*, 1903–4, 136.
123 *Ibid.*, 238–9.

so a choice would have to be made: some would be listed as indispensable, and others optional. The Syndicate had consulted widely: the schools had urged them to reduce the element in the examination which depended on the study of set books, begged them not to increase the number of subjects tested in the examination, and suggested that the examination in English might be more thorough. The Royal Society hoped that the examination would be reformed so as to encourage 'the study of Science in Schools'.[124]

Faced with this advice, the Syndicate proposed that the Previous Examination should be divided into three parts, all of which must be taken, though not necessarily at the same time, by all candidates for a degree, except in so far as they had obtained exemption from one or more of the parts. The third part was to consist of papers in English, scripture, history and science; the second part was to consist largely of the mathematical content of the current examination; but the first part was radically new: it was to consist of papers in classical Greek, Latin, French and German. Candidates had to offer two languages, and one of them had to be an ancient classical language. For the first time since 1822, when the Previous Examination was introduced, it would now be possible to offer either Greek or Latin, instead of having to do both. Despite the Syndicate's argument that in the twentieth century it was appropriate to allow students to choose one modern language rather than a second classical language, the proposal was perceived almost entirely as an attack on Greek. As such it went to the very heart of the idea of a liberal education for, as Sir Richard Jebb, the Regius Professor of Greek, was to urge, it was common ground that language and literature formed at least one indispensable element in a liberal education, and that Greek was,

> by the admission of a majority of educators, an incomparable instrument of linguistic and literary training . . . The literature of Greece had left a series of typical models both in verse and in prose. The Greek language was the most perfect vehicle of expression which the world had known. The Greek mind had been the great originating mind of Europe; fertile in ideas which were still fruitful in every field of knowledge, ideas which at the Renaissance exercised a powerful influence on the transition from the medieval to the modern world . . . No language, no literature, was at once so ancient and so intensely modern as the Greek.[125]

The formal Discussion of the Syndicate's Report was spread over three days. It contained some remarkable testimony about the place of Greek in a liberal education, not least being that of the distinguished medieval historian, F. W. Maitland, who was the Downing Professor of the Laws of England.[126] He confessed that, despite having had good teachers and a conventional classical education, he had never been cut out to

---

[124] *Ibid.*, 1904–5, 194.   [125] *Ibid.*, 356.   [126] *Ibid.*, 372–3.

learn Greek; and having been compelled to do so had conceived a great disgust of it. For he had never really

> learnt Greek, but one thing he did learn, namely, to hate Greek and its alphabet, and its accents, and its accidence, and its syntax, and its prosody, and all its appurtenances; to long for the day when he would be allowed to learn something else; to vow that if he ever got rid of that accursed thing never, never again would he open a Greek book or write a Greek word.

He believed that there were 'crowds of boys' just like him, and the 'hopeless drudgery' of learning the language had 'dulled and numbed their minds' as it dulled and numbed the minds of their masters. The trouble was the emphasis to the exclusion of all else on grammar; and to those who argued that that sort of Greek lay at the root of a humanist education, then let there be a new degree, Bachelor of Humanities, 'to be abbreviated as Hum.B.'. He was very sympathetic to those who put up the cry of leave well alone, but that had always been the cry of 'the craftsmen who made the silver shrines. Diana was just as good a goddess as another'. (Later Mr Giles would reply that Profesor Maitland was ungenerous to say publicly what was being whispered in private, that those supporting Greek did so 'because Greek supported them', and in any case was it not more noble to worship Diana of the Ephesians than the cult of Alexander the coppersmith?)[127] Maitland simply could not see how the survival of Greek was dependent on its being retained as a compulsory element in an examination:

> Just suppose that any representative of Natural Science, or any mere outsider such as he was, were to press home the argument that those two causes were bound up together, that the study of Greek after all these centuries of culture, that this beautiful plant was so sickly that it would droop and die unless it was tied to a stick, or a bundle of sticks; that their commerce with the ancients was obviously so unremunerative that it required the protection of a prohibitory tariff; that in order that the few might eat oysters the many must be crammed with powdered oyster-shells. Well, if that were so – he would see whether the roof of the Senate House would come down – he would say 'Let Greek perish, and let it perish everlastingly!'[128]

The President of Queens', who had had the 'somewhat perilous honour', of being the chairman of the Syndicate, had introduced the Report in more measured terms. He had not liked some of the detail in the Report, but he had become convinced of the necessity, in principle, to abandon compulsory Greek. The most important reason was that, increasingly, Greek was not being taught in the schools. Room was being made for sciences and modern languages, and the effect was to squeeze Greek out of the school-day.[129] Many speakers, while regretting that this was so, agreed that it was indeed the case, and that only the bigger and better-funded schools were able to

---

[127] *Ibid.*, 388.   [128] *Ibid.*, 373.   [129] *Ibid.*, 354–5.

maintain a full classical course. Even at schools where classics were quite secure there was unease. The Head Master of Winchester had submitted evidence to suggest that if the University did not bring in a more varied entrance examination reflecting more accurately what was being taught in the schools, then 'the tendency of boys and parents to regard education as complete without going to Oxford or Cambridge will grow' and they would look to other Universities.[130]

Sir George Young drew upon his experience as a Charity Commissioner responsible for re-organising secondary education in the country at large. He agreed that, almost without exception, Greek was excluded from the regular curriculum in most secondary schools, 'and from the curriculum in less well-endowed schools and those which had lower fees.'[131] It was wrong of Cambridge to retain a qualification in Greek and thus close the door of the University to the great majority of boys in the country: it was not only socially indefensible, but it was not in the best interests of the University either, because it was from the numerous ordinary schools up and down the country that the Newtons, Wordsworths and Whewells of the future were being nurtured.[132] Moreover, as the President of Queens' had pointed out, for some years the number of freshmen had been practically stationary. If the Senate refused to make any change to its entrance qualifications, then the University would run the risk of being deprived of students, would lose its 'rightful place' in higher education, and would go down before the competition of the new Universities. More serious was the risk of provoking reaction within Cambridge and compulsion from without, for

> such a course would end in revolution, and . . . their literary studies would be much more largely endangered. He was therefore persuaded that the truly conservative course was to recognise in time the working of educational forces, which they might perhaps be allowed to regret, but which it did not lie within their power to control, and to maintain and to forward a policy of sober and moderate reform.[133]

A number of the more distinguished classicists were prepared to follow this advice. The Master of Trinity (who had previously been the Head Master of Harrow) had no real fears for the survival of Greek. The great schools would continue to teach it; heads of families who cared about it would see that their sons were taught it; University prizes and scholarships would still be competed for; the work of introducing the genius of the Greek people to the mass of Englishmen and women through the means of translations was only just beginning; and the growing number of women 'who had received, either at Cambridge or elsewhere, the inestimable benefit of being initiated into the language of Greece would not forget, as a part of that inspiration which no Master could give with the same power as a mother, to make the language of Greece a matter of love and almost worship to their children.'[134] The Provost of King's took the

[130] Quoted *ibid.*, 399.   [131] *Ibid.*, 373.   [132] *Ibid.*, 374.   [133] *Ibid.*, 354.   [134] *Ibid.*, 364.

long historical view and reminded the Senate of how Greek had thrived at the University for many centuries before it had been made a compulsory part of the Previous Examination.[135] Dr Jackson, who had never regretted making the Greek language and literature his life's work, and who had taught those subjects at Cambridge for forty years, believed nonetheless that the study of Greek was right, but only 'for the right people. For the right people, it was the very best instrument; for the wrong people, it was the very worst.' The Syndicate had produced a Report which set about defining an entrance examination for the University in the clearest, boldest and best possible way. He wholeheartedly supported the changes proposed 'just because he was a believer in Greek literature and Greek thought'.[136] And Dr Peile, the Master of Christ's, who had proved so difficult over the reform of the Classical Tripos, stated firmly that 'if they at Cambridge hardened their hearts, and stiffened their necks, and refused to make any change, they would alienate from themselves the most progressive and the most actively-minded parts of the nation, who would look for leading to them no longer. They could not afford that.'[137]

However, the weight of emotion was on the other side of the debate. The Head Master of Nottingham High School was convinced that all the better-bred and stronger characters at his school were on the classical side (a point disputed by the Head Master of the Leys School with regard to *his* boys).[138] French and German were trivial languages to learn and no substitute as a test of scholarship for Greek: anyone of culture could acquire them on a tour to the continent (a point of view challenged by Dr Breul who did not think that the language of Luther and Lessing, of Goethe and Schiller, of Humboldt and Mommsen could 'be "picked up" during a few weeks' stay abroad').[139] But it was left to the incorrigible Professor Ridgeway to lay waste the Syndicate and all their works by saying all the unsayable things.

Ridgeway was in no doubt that the assault on Greek must be repulsed. If classics were in a bad way it was because they were so badly taught, not least by Dr Jackson and Dr Peile, and by masters in the schools. That should be remedied before the University changed its rule. The Senate were being asked to give up something of importance for the most cowardly of reasons: people outside the University wanted change; well, it was not the duty of the University to give in to them. They were not fighting the cause of Greek and Latin alone (for he was sure if Greek fell, Latin would follow soon thereafter), 'but the cause of literary education as a whole, and they were not fighting it against the higher scientific side at all, but against the scientific nonentities, and the commercial scientists'. It was ridiculous to say that people outside knew better than the dons what the University was all about: 'Was the brain going to lead or the tail?' And they must not be frightened 'by any mutterings or rumblings of what might

[135] *Ibid.*, 389–90.   [136] *Ibid.*, 395–7.   [137] *Ibid.*, 388.   [138] *Ibid.*, 362, 371.
[139] *Ibid.*, 382.

16   Henry Montagu Butler, DD (1833–1918), by Sir William Orpen.
Montagu Butler was admitted to Trinity College as a pensioner in 1850. He
was elected a scholar in 1853, won the Browne Medal in 1854 and the Porson
Prize in 1855, and was also President of the Union Society. He was appointed
Head Master of Harrow School in 1859, Dean of Gloucester in 1885 and Master
of Trinity in 1886. He was a keen supporter of education for women, being for
some years a member of the Council of Girton College, and he was in the
forefront of the campaign for admitting women to the titles of degrees in 1897.

This portrait was given to Trinity in 1911.

happen to them if they did not do what was wanted'. All this needless controversy had been stirred by the simple fact that there was a move afoot to get money for the University. 'The millionnaires were being hunted down in all directions. Springes were being laid for the woodcocks by all kinds of people in the University, but the woodcocks would not be caught.' The Senate were being told that no one would do anything for Cambridge 'so long as it was regarded as a monkish place, full of dead languages, and so forth'. But Ridgeway was sceptical as to whether money would come with change. Those who had given to the Universities at Manchester and Liverpool and the like did so because they had made their money there and their families had been in those places for generations. 'They planted down money because it gave them fame. It marked their names. Probably they wished to be made peers.' Similar developments could be seen in America.

> Did they believe that if they turned the University of Cambridge inside out such men would give them anything? They stood no more chance than of getting money from the Corporation of Cambridge. But because of these things they had the Syndicate setting down the regulations of all the mushroom Universities to show them what they ought to do. Did they believe that by making their ancient University like those young Universities they were going to survive the struggle between the two classes of Universities? Nothing of the kind. It was by being able to give people who come to Cambridge something of a higher quality than they could get elsewhere that they were going to survive; and that is what he hoped and trusted and believed would be the case, and that they would give them the highest form of literary culture combined with the highest form of scientific advance.

It was absurd to suggest that the University become a 'glorified technical college. They could not compete with Birmingham. Would the Corporation of Cambridge give them £250,000 to set up brewing and metallurgy?' He had no patience with the problems of so-called practical men. It was they who had neglected to take advantage of what the University had been able to offer for many years. 'They had shut their eyes too long to what science could do for manufacturers. There had been slumbering in business, lack of enterprise, and dishonesty which had led them to push bad things abroad.' It was no use blaming the University for these shortcomings and the Senate should not be moved by the cry that Cambridge had done nothing for the world of business.

Then Ridgeway turned his scorn on to the Master of Trinity. Dr Butler was an honest man and had not pretended that things were better than they were. The Master's picture of the future was one where Greek would fade away, and he had not said otherwise. He had relied on certain feeble things to keep the classics alive — translations, prizes and scholarships, being instilled with a love of Greek at the mother's breast — but none of these would really do and the classics would die and with

17 Sir William Ridgeway (1853–1926) came of a Devon family which settled
in Ulster under James I – 'all first-class fighting men'. He was educated at
Trinity College Dublin, Peterhouse and Gonville and Caius College. He was
Professor of Greek at University College, Cork, from 1883 until his election to
the Disney Professorship of Archaeology and a Fellowship at Caius in 1892.
The Disney Chair was not well endowed and Ridgeway was also appointed to
the newly established Brereton Readership in Classics in 1907. His entry in the
Dictionary of National Biography records with masterly understatement that
'his affection for the Anglican Church and for the traditions of Cambridge
scholarship limited his enthusiasm for reform'.

them 'the great glory of the literary side of the University would be gone for ever'. What the Senate must do was to

> stand firm. Let them fight for the battle of free literature. Let them see to it that the old languages which had been the best instruments of active thought that the world had known were still taught. Let them supplement them by French and German in the schools . . . Let them make Science compulsory in the schools, so as to have a complete harmonising blend for the literary man and the scientific man.

Then should anyone enquire into the University they would see that the scientific schools were 'simply bristling with activity, and the literary schools showing ever-increasing signs of vigour, [and] they would say that they were doing well, and ought to be left alone'.[140] Faced with this barrage of criticism, the Syndicate went away to amend their Report. In a revised version, published in February 1905, they made a number of concessions of a minor and technical nature; but they held fast to the principle that only one classical language should be compulsory in the Previous Examination. On Friday and Saturday the 3rd and 4th of March, the Vice-Chancellor presided over the voting in the Senate-House. The turn-out was high – around 2,500; and the result was quite clear: the main proposal that a new Previous Examination be instituted was defeated by 1,527 votes to 1,063, and all the associated Graces fell by a similar margin. But all was not quite over. Although the resident dons were divided on this issue, it seems that a fair number of them were prepared to contemplate the change proposed. An analysis of the vote published in November 1905 made it clear that the Graces had been lost 'by the decisive weight of non-resident clergymen, who came up *en masse*' to vote against the Syndicate's proposals. Had the voting been confined either to laymen, or to resident members of the Senate, then the proposals would have been carried.[141]

A second report of the Studies Syndicate followed in March 1906. This attempted to find a compromise: the Syndicate now argued for distinguishing between those students following 'literary courses' and those students following 'scientific courses'. There would be different requirements for each, and significantly those studying science would be compelled to offer only one classical language. This was regarded by some as a bold step 'and great will be the questionings aroused both by the principle itself and by the difficulty of arranging the various studies under these two sharply divided sections'. The ink was hardly dry on the *Reporter* before people began to wonder why moral sciences should be a literary study but economics a scientific one;

---

140 *Ibid.*, 368–70.
141 *Ibid*, 641–4. *CR*, 9 November 1905, 60. Oxford had earlier, and with much less fuss, also agreed by 200 votes to 164, to retain Greek. *Ibid.*, 1 December 1904, 98.

and when it came to the vote the new package 'died a tame and uninteresting death' being lost by 746 votes to 241.[142]

The reformers had been unwise to try and put their case again so soon after such a decisive vote; and their analysis of the part played in their defeat by the non-resident clergy had come across as mean and petty: it was certainly counter-productive in holding together their own support. It had not helped, either, that the Michaelmas term of 1905 had seen the largest entry of freshmen ever recorded. But perhaps the wisest comment came from the pen of an 'ultra-Tory parson' who, after berating the radicals for stirring the anti-clerical pot, argued that

> causes which are fought with beating of drums and sending the fiery cross round the country are seldom really important, and never beneficial. What is wanted is steady reform brought about by wise legislation. Most people in Cambridge can be got to work together with a little judicious management, and the recommendations of Syndicates, chosen without party spirit, are as a rule accepted gratefully by the University.[143]

Besides, every reform would eventually have its day, even if the time for it had passed.

ઢ

Cambridge was not, in fact, irredeemably conservative in what it taught. The regulations in *Ordinances* might appear to lay down a rigid curriculum and determine what was examined, but the inspired teacher had plenty of room for manoeuvre within the rules. And often after long and bitter wrangles quite minor changes of regulation led to major creative explosions within the subjects themselves. Such movements were continually taking place in the old subjects – particularly in classics and mathematics – where everyone felt they had both knowledge and interest in how scholarship ought to be protected and developed. But it was common in newer subjects also; and although nothing was done without surviving challenge, hardly a year went by without some attempt at modification to one Tripos or another. Beneath a conservative, indeed reactionary, rhetoric, there was also a liberal pragmatism to admit change once it could be seen as a 'steady reform brought about by wise legislation'. It had also to withstand the scatter-shot of the non-placets: thus came about the Economic Tripos.

In the spring of 1902, Alfred Marshall, the Professor of Political Economy, organised a Memorial to the Council asking for the appointment of a Syndicate 'to enquire into and report upon the best means of enlarging the opportunities for the study in Cambridge of Economics and associated branches of Political Science'. The Memorial was a weighty one, attracting 130 signatures including five Heads of

---

[142] *Reporter 1905–6*, 586–90, 989. *CR*, 15 March 1906, 312; 31 May 1906, 428.
[143] *CR*, 9 November 1905, 60.

73

Houses, two Bishops and fourteen Professors, and a Syndicate was duly established to look into the matter. At that time, the only way of studying economics or politics was to take papers in economic history in the Historical Tripos or to take papers in political philosophy in the Moral Sciences Tripos. But, as the Report of the Syndicate pointed out, this was no longer good enough, given the increasing importance and complexity of economic issues, and their close connection with politics. Universities in the United States and in Germany had long offered serious courses of study on economics and politics, and even in this country London, Birmingham, Manchester, Leeds and Liverpool were beginning to mount undergraduate courses in the subject. Cambridge, the Syndicate argued, should advance in the same way, partly to have a voice in developing the economics at a professional academic level, partly to play a role in the education of men going into business and public life and partly to lessen the 'risk of the alienation of English business men from the Universities'. The solution proposed was a simple one: there should be a new Tripos and a new Board of Studies to supervise it.[144]

During the Discussion, many of the standard arguments against innovation were trotted out. Dr Cunningham, the economic historian, was against a new Tripos because no serious economics could be undertaken other than by reference to history and philosophy. J. E. McTaggart, the philosopher, was against it because he did not believe that Professor Marshall would be able to find the money to run a new course of study successfully, and even if he could, he doubted whether it would be wise to accept it: economists were bound to be asked to advise governments and politicians and so there was a great risk of political interference in the affairs of the University. Even Henry Jackson thought that yet another Tripos complete with committee to look after it was not what Cambridge wanted at the time.[145]

Around the Colleges the debate was joined as the parties mustered strength for the vote. One supporter of the new Tripos was filled with 'astonishment and amazement' at the ingenuity of members of the Senate 'in discovering reasons for not doing things', and, to add 'to the gaiety of nations', he uncovered the workings of the non-placet mind:[146]

Opposition Arguments

1. That the proposal is a new one.
2. That it is therefore a bad one.
3. That it is asked for by people outside.
4. That it is not asked for by people outside.
5. That if it were, that would be all the more reason why they should not have it.
6. That the members of the Syndicate are amiable and well-meaning people.

[144] *Reporter* 1902–3, 528–38. [145] *Ibid.*, 763–4. [146] *CR*, 21 May 1903, 314–15.

7. That the members of the Syndicate are ---------.
8. That the British Constitution is nothing if not ancient.
9. That the middle class is being squeezed out of existence.
10. That all Political Economy is contained in Mr Gladstone's speeches. Or if not, why not?
11. That there is really a great deal in what Dr M ---- says.
12. That the proposed Tripos is too narrow.
13. That it is too broad.
14. That it is too practical.
15. That it is not practical enough.
16. That the University is poor.
17. That it would be very dangerous to do anything that might tend to attract endowments to the University.
18. That Mr Carnegie never studied Economics.
19. Neither did Mr Pierpont Morgan.
20. That ----is a genius, and his opinions must therefore be worthless.
21. That ----is not a genius, and his opinions must therefore, etc.
22. That there ought to be a comma after the word ---- in Regulation ---- line ----.
23. That Economics ought to be spelt with a small e.
24. That people are more interested in their souls than in their stomachs.
25. That if they aren't they ought to be.
26. That you can't arrange one student in three classes.
27. That if you could, he would be none the better for it.
28. That everyone would take the new Tripos.
29. That no one would take it.
30. That anyhow we aren't going to be bullied by any Syndicate. That we intend to vote against this, and any other scheme that might be brought forward. But that no one is more anxious than we are that the study of Economics should be developed in the University. And that altogether it's a great pity.

Such a litany of impossible, though perversely plausible, argument blights the hopes of any would-be reformer: it seems so unfair that while there is only one reason for doing something (namely that it is right to do it), there should be so many reasons for not doing it. The economists had, however, marshalled their troops well, and a Grace establishing the new Tripos found 103 dons on the South side of the Senate-House to only 76 on the North side.[147]

On the whole, though, the opening years of the new century found Cambridge in a profoundly conservative mood; no doubt the strain of making changes told and there was a strong desire to stand fast if possible: some change good, no change better, as the typical don might have put it. But the mood in the country was for change. December

[147] *Reporter 1902–3*, 963–4.

1906 had seen the great Liberal landslide in the Parliamentary elections and the installation of Campbell-Bannerman's reforming government. By 1907 more of the dons, if not vigorously proposing radical reform, were at least reconciled to the fact that, as one wit had put it a little earlier on, they could not always 'atone for the busy indolence of term by the employment of their vacations in complete rest'.[148] On 25 July, Dr Gore, the Bishop of Birmingham, clearly in cahoots with a group of Oxford dons ('well-known cranks, with archaeological or other axes to grind'[149] who published a letter in the *Times* on the same day about the same subject), asked the House of Lords whether, given the changes that had taken place in education since the 1870s, and the difficulties which the two old universities seemed to have in coming to grips with things, it might not be a good idea to have a Royal Commission to sort them out.

Dr Gore mounted a familiar radical attack: Oxford and Cambridge were out of touch with the nation; their money was not spent helping poor scholars; and 'they were to far too great a degree the playgrounds of the nation'. The Bishop of Bristol, being a good Cambridge man, made an immediate defence of his own University at least, pointing out that it was fully up-to-date in all the fashionable modern studies, managed its resources well and all that was needed for it to play its full part in contemporary society was an extra £75,000 a year. The University's own formal response awaited the Vice-Chancellor's speech to the Senate in October. He left the matter until the end, firmly rejecting the notion of further external interference in Cambridge and its Colleges. The University neither desired nor feared yet another Royal Commission, but, E. S. Roberts said, with masterly understatement, 'I believe that there is hardly a single suggested change which could not be effected by existing statutory powers, by internal re-organisation, and by the co-operation of Colleges.'[150]

The Bishop of Birmingham's criticisms may have been unfair. Much, after all, had been achieved at Cambridge in recent years. Heroic efforts had been made to fund science, and the vast building sites in Downing Street, together with the proliferation of science teachers, showed that they had not been in vain. The search for new endowment, under the leadership of the Chancellor, had provided some new financial resources, and the University and Colleges continually squeezed out money from here and there to fund things considered necessary or desirable. New courses, like economics, had been successfully introduced. The Mathematics Tripos had seen a major overhaul allowing it, among other things, to take more account of the interests of physics and engineering. The Colleges were co-operating more and more in the provision of teaching – even in mathematics: Trinity in the Michaelmas term of 1907 abandoned its position of proud isolation and arranged with King's, Caius and Clare a

---

[148] *CR*, 9 May 1901, 293.   [149] *Ibid.*, 17 October 1907, 2.   [150] *Ibid.*

joint scheme of mathematical lectures for the undergraduates of all four Colleges. Such arrangements had become much more the norm in classics. In the newer subjects, there was a realistic appreciation that teaching was effectively provided for all students by those who held University office.

But there were also frustrations. New money did not adequately meet new needs, and both University and Colleges felt increasingly under financial pressure. Not much progress was being made to solve the problems of the University Library: shortages of space, staff and endowment were recognised as underlying difficulties, but because every member of the Senate had an opinion about the shortcomings of the library and what should be done about them, insuperable political difficulties emerged for every solution proposed. The Senate had also rejected proposals giving full membership of the University to women and denied recognition of St Edmund's as a Public Hostel. Tripos reforms generally tended to have difficulty in passing through the Senate and largely non-resident votes had doomed the proposal that competence in Greek, as well as in Latin, should no longer be considered a necessary precondition for sitting the examinations for a Cambridge degree. Reform of classics, recognised by everyone as being necessary, had divided the resident teachers on points of detail and consequently many of the younger dons, of whom Cornford was one, had felt that an opportunity for major improvement of the Tripos had been lost. Not surprisingly, these frustrations, allied with renewed criticism from without, encouraged renewed speculation on how Cambridge might be reformed.

A straw in the wind came early in the Michaelmas term. A by-election for three seats on the Council of the Senate produced an unusual result. None of the successful candidates had ever served on the Council before and they were not particularly identified as belonging to any of the existing factions. 'Perhaps young Cambridge is making itself felt', ran an editorial in the *Cambridge Review*, 'and at no distant date the Geological Museum and the Council of the Senate may no longer be appropriately used as synonymous for a receptacal of fossils'.[151] Throughout the term, the journal carried articles about what might be done. The threat from Democracy might be countered by increasing the provision for the working classes by setting up a Cambridge equivalent of Ruskin College at Oxford and by adding to the existing number of diplomas that could be taken without having to be resident or to pass ordinary University examinations. A more vigorous programme of extra-mural studies might be developed, with new lecturers, appointed by both the University and Colleges, going out to meet the demand for learning from working men in Newcastle, Sunderland, Middlesbrough, York, Derby, Leicester, Northampton and numerous other towns. A full-blooded scheme of rationalisation was advocated by A. I. Tillyard at half-term.

[151] *Ibid.*, 24 October 1907, 24.

Colleges should be grouped into larger, more efficient, units; there should be a single body to oversee both University and College teaching; there should be one Board 'doing the administrative work of both University and Colleges, *i.e.*, discharging the duties of the Financial Board and of Bursars, Stewards and Tutors, so far as these last are concerned with money matters'. There should be a Vice-Chancellor who was not a Head of House, and he should have a salary and an official residence. The Council of the Senate should be chosen from all members of the Senate, without any restrictions; and there should be a way of seeking formally help from men who were in touch with the outside world. There should be proper entrance examinations, in which Greek would only figure as an optional subject, and Tripos courses should be simplified so that undergraduates could enter at eighteen and go out into the world at twenty-one. There should be a development of post-graduate studies and research work, to be the responsibility of the Professors. And all Fellowships should be attached to offices, administrative, or educational, or tied to research.[152]

This was heady stuff, and the editors of the *Review*, no doubt seeking to redress the balance, published a piece by an undergraduate which, while admitting that junior members did not very much 'trouble their heads about' University reform, nevertheless urged that the Colleges should not be interfered with; that candidates for the ordinary BA degree should not be discouraged since 'an occasional infiltration of less brilliant people' made Colleges more interesting and, besides, 'saves us from priggishness'; and that, most important of all, no one should think of taking away any of the powers and privileges of the non-resident MAs to act as the final arbiters of University affairs since it was vital to have a check on the resident members of the Senate – 'a body of men, which is much too clever to inspire fully the confidence of the English, from entering upon schemes, prompted by the noblest idealism, but almost certain to be unfortunate in their results'. Even so, from the point of view of the undergraduate, that most conservative of the species in the University, there was a case for better co-ordination of lectures, the abolition of a few prize fellowships and improvements to College kitchens.[153] Another correspondent gaily suggested that since the University's problems were financial, a practical solution to the difficulty lay in having the Proctors levy fines according to the capacity of culprits to pay – 'by the seizure of one wealthy undergraduate, capless or fumigant, he [the Proctor] might in one moment gain what was formerly a year's profit. And if he caught, for example, a foreign potentate, he might ask what he would, even up to half of his kingdom, and the University Chest would cop the swag.' In addition, thought might be given to treating Girton and Newnham as Henry VIII had dealt with the monasteries – confiscate their buildings and revenues for the benefit of the University.[154]

152 *Ibid.*, 7 November 1907, 64–5.   153 *Ibid.*, 14 November 1907, 81–2.
154 *Ibid.*, 16 January 1908, 166.

The desire to do new and daring things rippled throughout the whole life of the University that Michaelmas term. There had long been protestations that Cambridge theatre did not cater adequately for those who loved good drama, particularly Elizabethan plays. But on 11 and 12 November at the ADC theatre was staged a performance of Marlowe's *Dr Faustus*. Handbills had circulated advertising the event; but it was known in advance that there was something a bit odd about it: for one thing, although speculation had been rife as to which members of the University had been cast in the roles of the Seven Deadly Sins, 'if it be true, as we hear, that the programme is to contain no names, our curiosity, unless we can see through the make-up, will have to go unsatisfied'.[155] And so it proved.

> It was a queer performance. The older generation were scandalised almost before the play began: no scenery, only dingy green hangings [hired from Eaden Lilleys for £3 5s 10d], no music, no footlights, frequent 'black-outs', no names of actors printed. And all this in the A.D.C. Theatre, with its familiar portraits, its familiar memories! No wonder they were upset by it all. '*Faustus* isn't a play at all' – 'absurd for undergraduates to attempt tragedy' – 'why didn't they get someone with experience to coach them?' – 'why do they act in the dark?' – 'not always in very nice taste' – it was indeed a queer performance. Faustus looked absurdly young; Mephistophilis, his face completely hidden by his cowl, generally turned his back to the audience, and spoke in a thick and indistinct voice which often served merely as a backdrop to the piercing whispers of the Master of ---, whose thirst for information was insatiable. But in spite of these things and many others . . . the play had a new spirit of its own.[156]

We now know, of course, that Rupert Brooke played Mephistophilis; the performances were a financial as well as an artistic success, and the ensuing weeks witnessed the birth of the Marlowe Society, committed 'to perform Elizabethan and other plays and to study the drama with a view to such performances'. It was an elite activity and productions were to be staged in the Michaelmas term 'in such years as there is no Greek play'.[157] Francis Cornford was the Society's Senior Treasurer.

But it was harder to give practical and permanent shape to the wish for University reform. After all, the whole constitution was designed to prevent change in so far as possible; and those to whom the Bishop of Birmingham and Mr Tillyard appeared nightly in dreams as wild destroyers of the universe knew as they savoured their port and stilton in Senior Combination Rooms that they had only to sit tight and the frenzy would pass. Besides, already by 14 November, the suggestion was bruited abroad that given the need to proceed with caution, and only in the light of considering in full all

[155] *Ibid.*, 7 November 1907, 63.
[156] Edward J. Dent, 'Rupert Brooke', *The Cambridge Magazine*, 8 May 1915, 390; and the programme for the Marlowe Society's production of Tamburlaine, Cambridge Arts Theatre, 9–13 March 1993. I am indebted to Timothy Cribb for help on this point.
[157] *CR*, 6 February 1908, 208–9.

18 Francis Henry John Jenkinson (1853–1923), by John Singer Sargent. Jenkinson was a classical scholar, entomologist and antiquarian. He went up to Trinity in 1872 and was elected a Fellow in 1878. University Librarian 1889–1923. The portrait was commissioned in 1915 to commemorate Jenkinson's twenty-fifth year as Librarian.

the relevant information, then the thing to do was to appoint a Syndicate 'consisting of men thoroughly acquainted not only with the working of University and College affairs, but with the finances, *materiel* and *personnel* of these bodies'. Among the duties of such a Syndicate would be to report to the Senate on what reforms, no doubt, if any, were necessary. [158]

In fact, the only real political sport played during the term of reform came at the very end and concerned the rules for the election of the University Librarian. Appointment to high University office had in many cases been made by large bodies of men. The election of the Librarian still lay with the whole Senate. Two names would be proposed by the Council and an appointment made by vote of the Senate. But just as some of the Professorships were now being increasingly appointed to by small Boards of Electors who knew something about the subject of the chair concerned, so too came the proposal that the Librarian should be elected by a specialist committee. This was justified on the grounds that 'the systematic management of Libraries has developed so much of recent years as to become a science in itself; and the present mode of election does not give sufficient security that the person elected will be thoroughly familiar with the most approved methods of managing a large public Library'. [159]

'Those who dislike and distrust democratic methods will rejoice at the proposal' commented the *Cambridge Review*, pointing out that the proposed membership of the special Board of Electors 'seems to fulfil every requirement of a benevolent oligarchy, as eight of its ten members are to be members of the two bodies which nominate to it, the Council of the Senate and the Library Syndicate'. The remaining two members of the proposed Board were to be non-residents to allow for the 'addition to the electoral body of some persons who have special knowledge of the best modern methods of Library management'. [160] The upholders of the privileges of the Senate were outraged. Archdeacon Cunningham organised a fly sheet to non-placet the proposal. He argued, first, that

> all elections *in camera* preclude the possibility of effective criticism, and secondly, that these considerations apply with especial force to the Librarianship for 'experts' in all the other great libraries of England would possibly only be able to exercise their expertness in the University Library by bringing it into line with those other libraries: *i.e.*, by seriously curtailing the present privileges of members of the Senate.

And he ended with 'an opportune reference to the unsuitable nature of the present time for such a proposal: can we expect subscriptions to keep coming in from the general public of the University as we diminish public privileges and lessen public control?' [161]

[158] *Ibid.*, 14 November 1907, 84.   [159] *Reporter 1907–8*, 334–5.   [160] *CR*, 23 January 1908, 176.
[161] *Ibid.*, 13 February 1908, 226. 'It seems curious that, at a time when the University is seeking closer links with its wider membership and is hoping for their financial support, it should think it wise to detract from their status and privileges.' Remarks made by T. N. Milner in the Discussion held on 13 July 1993 on the Third Report of the Statute and Ordinances Revision Syndicate; W. P. Kirkman also echoed Cunningham's last point: *Reporter 1992–3*, 1016, 1020.

The proposal was carried, a signal triumph of reform, by 54 votes to 4. [162]

But it was Cornford who, on the very eve of publication of *Microcosmographia Academica*, went right to the political heart of the matter: [163]

Quis Custodiet?:

When nominees have nominees
    Behind their backs, to bite 'em,
And these again are nominees,
    You get ad infinitum.

The Syndicate you cannot trust,
    Because the Council chose 'em;
Their taste, the Syndics say, is bad,
    As he can see who knows 'em.

The Council say, at choosing men
    The Senate are not clever;
Witness themselves – the argument,
    You see, goes on for ever.

Or does it stop at Senators,
    Who've none behind, to bite 'em?
They are not nominees at all:
    We've *got* ad infinitum.

But can they trust *themselves* to choose
    A bibliothecary?
If all their nominees are bad,
    To *elect* they should be chary.

But if their nominees are good,
    The Council must be fit 'uns
To choose at least a Syndicate
    Of ordinary Britons.

And these, it follows, must be fit
    (So argues Aristotle)
To choose a man to dust the books
    And little flies to bottle.

When nominees have nominees,
    And so ad infinitum,
The argument gets round behind
    Your own poor backs, to bite 'em.

છ

[162] *Reporter 1907–8*, 603.   [163] *CR*, 13 February 1908, 244.

In many respects, it requires a real effort of the historical imagination to conjure up the Cambridge of the young Francis Cornford; but despite the colossal changes wrought by the twentieth century it is remarkable how much of the old Cambridge survives. Now there are thirty-one Colleges, of various shapes and sizes, and hardly any of the undergraduates leave Cambridge without an honours degree. Each year, around 1,300 papers are set in a greatly expanded range of examinations.[164] The University is in charge of teaching, research has become much more important and the General Board of the Faculties is acknowledged as the key to much of Cambridge's academic business – so the Master of Caius, wearing his College cap, was right to be angry about the institution of a Board of General Studies.

The Senate has been replaced by the Regent House as the watchdog of liberty and the bastion of conservatism. This consists of around 3,000 people, and most are too busy to take much of an interest in University affairs except when they are upset. We are still, many say, governed 'very badly', but that does not seem to affect the University's capacity to achieve academic distinction. The dons do not have to be so public about their votes as once they were; and in some cases may even vote by postal ballot: so only on deconstructive occasions do the non-placets have to remember which side of the Senate-House lies to the north.[165] A Vice-Chancellor with a house of his own is almost the only one of Tillyard's proposals of 1907 to have come into effect, and that not until Michaelmas 1992, though about every twenty years a Syndicate set up to reform the University from within has put forward all his other schemes. King's Parade may now be given over to trucks and French school-children; but for all who read Cornford's *Microcosmographia* it will symbolise for ever the hard truth that the most important decisions are fixed outside the meeting.

It is hard to conceive of the University any more as part of the Church of England; but no College Chapels have closed their doors and John Piper's window in the newest at Robinson College is as glorious as that to adorn any twentieth-century cathedral. Selwyn became a full College in 1957, and elected its first layman as Master in 1983; St Edmund's followed suit in 1985; but the Fellows of Queens' elected a Clerk in holy orders at their last election. The University is now more truly 'Mixed' as since the 1970s women have moved into all the men's Colleges; but they remain numerically weak at senior levels and still fall short of true equality in our byzantine system of

---

[164] 1,312 papers were sat in 1991–2; 1,287 in 1992–3. I owe this information to Mr R. F. Holmes.

[165] As happened, quite exceptionally, on 16 May 1992 when voting was held to determine whether or not to award an honorary degree of Doctor of Letters to M. Jacques Derrida. The voting was 336 placet; 204 non-placet (*Reporter* 1991–2, 684). The flysheets circulated on that occasion are reprinted *ibid.*, 685–8. One of the leading opponents of the proposal, Howard Erskine-Hill, wrote an account of the affair from this point of view in *CR*, vol. 113, number 2319, December 1991, 173–7; this was followed by 'Reflections on the "Derrida Affair"', *CR*, vol. 114, number 2320, 25–36.

government, that is: 'half the representation on any committee, and half of *them* incompetent'. [166]

The Registry no longer publishes a learned treatise every year, but stands at the head of a civil service running into hundreds. They occupy the whole and more of the buildings once the domain of the University Library. The eastern quadrangle of the Old Schools is still without an elegant canopy of glass and wrought iron, but it has of late sprouted huts to protect the clerks of the Financial Board from inclement weather: a great desecration, Professor Ridgeway's ghost wails, but at least he can still wind in and out of the colonnade. [167] The Librarian now has more to do than dust the books and bottle little flies; but he needs a new building or two and the grace to be patient with the baying of the Adullamites: the little world is just as vibrant and exciting, just as mean and vexatious as it ever was, still in need of the company of Cornford's clean and humorous intellect.

[166] Conversation with Joanna Womack while walking up and down King's Parade Michaelmas term 1991.
[167] The huts disappeared while this text was at the printer.

84

MICROCOSMOGRAPHIA ACADEMICA  BEING A GUIDE FOR THE YOUNG ACADEMIC POLITICIAN

By F. M. Cornford

UNIVERSITY
LIBRARY
CAMBRIDGE

BOWES AND BOWES, CAMBRIDGE
MCMVIII

TO

EDWARD GRANVILLE BROWNE

PREFACE TO THE SECOND EDITION

THERE was a time towards the end of 1914, when many people imagined that after the war human nature, in our part of the world, would be different. They even thought it would be better in some ways. I have an idea that I shared in this illusion. But my friends who are still active in this microcosm tell me that academic human nature, at any rate, remains true to the ancient type. Moreover, a short and inglorious career in the home forces and in a Government department has convinced me that the academic species is only one member of a genus wider than I had supposed. Frequenters of the Church Congress, too, have admitted that they sometimes turn to the pages of this guide for help. Considering all this, I have persuaded the publishers to reprint it as it stands.

I fancy (though I am not sure) that there is just one feature of academic life that has become a little more prominent since the war. If I could have recaptured the mood of the fortnight in which this book was written, I might have added a chapter on Propaganda, defined as that branch of the art of lying which consists in very nearly deceiving your friends without quite deceiving your enemies. But the subject is not yet ripe for treatment; the art is still imperfect. We must leave it to be worked out by the party whose mission it is to keep the university safe for aristo-democracy.

October 1922   F. M. C.

ADVERTISEMENT

If you are young, do not read this book; it is not fit for you;
If you are old, throw it away; you have nothing to learn from it;
If you are unambitious, light the fire with it; you do not need its guidance.

But, if you are neither less than twenty-five years old, nor more than thirty;
And, if you are ambitious withal, and your spirit hankers after academic politics;
Read, and may your soul (if you have a soul) find mercy!

I WARNING

'Any one of us might say, that although in words he is not able to meet you at each
step of the argument, he sees as a fact that academic persons, when they carry on study,
not only in youth as a part of education, but as the pursuit of their maturer years, most of
them become decidedly queer, not to say rotten; and that those who may be considered
the best of them are made useless to the world by the very study which you extol.
   'Well, and do you think that those who say so are wrong?
   'I cannot tell, he replied; but I should like to know what is your opinion?
   'Hear my answer; I am of opinion that they are quite right.'

PLATO, Republic VI

My heart is full of pity for you, O young academic politician. If you *will* be a
politician, you have a painful path to follow, even though it be a short one, before you
nestle down into a modest incompetence. While you are young you will be oppressed,
and angry, and increasingly disagreeable. When you reach middle age, at five-and-
thirty, you will become complacent, and, in your turn, an oppressor; those whom you
oppress will find you still disagreeable; and so will all the people whose toes you trod
upon in youth. It will seem to you then that you grow wiser every day, as you learn
more and more of the reasons why things should not be done, and understand more
fully the peculiarities of powerful persons, which make it quixotic even to attempt
them without first going through an amount of squaring and lobbying sufficient to
sicken any but the most hardened soul. If you persist to the threshold of old age—your
fiftieth year, let us say—you will be a powerful person yourself, with an accretion of
peculiarities which other people will have to study in order to square you. The toes you
will have trodden on by this time will be as the sands of the sea-shore; and from far
below you will mount the roar of a ruthless multitude of young men in a hurry. You
may perhaps grow to be aware what they are in a hurry to do. They are in a hurry to get
you out of the way.

   O young academic politicians, my heart is full of pity for you now; but when you are
old, if you will stand in the way, there will be no more pity for you than you deserve;
and that will be none at all.

   I shall take it that you are in the first flush of ambition, and just beginning to make
yourself disagreeable. You think (do you not?) that you have only to state a reasonable
case, and people must listen to reason and act upon it at once. It is just this conviction

93

that makes you so unpleasant. There is little hope of dissuading you; but has it occurred to you that nothing is ever done until every one is convinced that it ought to be done, and has been convinced for so long that it is now time to do something else? And are you not aware that conviction has never yet been produced by an appeal to reason, which only makes people uncomfortable? If you want to move them, you must address your arguments to prejudice and to the political motive, which I will presently describe. I should hesitate to write down so elementary a principle, if I were not sure you need to be told it. And you will not believe me, because you think your cases are so much more reasonable than mine can have been, and you are ashamed to study men's weaknesses and prejudices. You would rather batter away at the Shield of Faith than spy out the joints in the harness.

I like you the better for your illusions; but it cannot be denied that they prevent you from being effective, and if you do not become effective before you cease to want anything to be done—why, what will be the good of you? So I present you with this academic microcosmography—the merest sketch of the little world that lies before you. A satirist or an embittered man might have used darker colours; and I own that I have only drawn those aspects which it is most useful that you, as a politician, should know. There is another world within this microcosm—a silent, reasonable world, which you are now bent on leaving. Some day you may go back to it; and you will enjoy its calm the more for your excursion in the world of unreason.

Now, listen, and I will tell you what this outer world is like.

II PARTIES

First, perhaps, I had better describe the parties in academic politics; it is not easy to distinguish them precisely. There are five; and they are called Conservative Liberals, Liberal Conservatives, Non-placets, Adullamites, and Young Men in a Hurry.

A *Conservative Liberal* is a broad-minded man, who thinks that something ought to be done, only not anything that anyone now desires, but something which was not done in 1881–82.

A *Liberal Conservative* is a broad-minded man, who thinks that something ought to be done, only not anything that anyone now desires; and that most things which were done in 1881–82 ought to be undone.

The men of both these parties are alike in being open to conviction; but so many convictions have already got inside, that it is very difficult to find the openings. They dwell in the Valley of Indecision.

The *Non-Placet* differs in not being open to conviction: he is a man of principle. A principle is a rule of inaction, which states a valid general reason for not doing in any particular case what, to unprincipled instinct, would appear to be right. The Non-placet believes that it is always well to be on the Safe Side, which can be easily located as the northern side of the interior of the Senate House. He will be a person whom you have never seen before, and will never see again anywhere but in his favourite station on the left of the place of judgment.

The *Adullamites* are dangerous, because they know what they want; and that is, all the money there is going. They inhabit a series of caves near Downing Street. They say to one another, 'If you will scratch my back, I will scratch yours; and if you won't, I will scratch your face.' It will be seen that these cave-dwellers are not refined, like classical men. That is why they succeed in getting all the money there is going.

A *Young Man in a Hurry* is a narrow-minded and ridiculously youthful prig, who is inexperienced enough to imagine that something might be done before very long, and even to suggest definite things. His most dangerous defect being want of experience, everything should be done to prevent him from taking any part in affairs. He may be known by his propensity to organise societies for the purpose of making silk purses out of sows' ears. This tendency is not so dangerous as it might seem; for it may be observed that the sows, after taking their washing with a grunt or two, trundle back unharmed to the wallow; and the purse-market is quoted as firm. The Young Man in a Hurry is afflicted with a conscience, which is apt to break out, like the measles, in patches. To listen to him, you would think he united the virtues of a Brutus to the passion for lost causes of a Cato; he has not learnt that most of his causes are lost by letting the Cato out of the bag, instead of tying him up firmly and sitting on him, as experienced people do.

O young academic politician, know thyself!

III CAUCUSES

A Caucus is like a mouse-trap: when you are outside you want to get in; and when you are inside the mere sight of the other mice makes you want to get out. The trap is baited with muffins and cigars—except in the case of the Non-placet Caucus, an ascetic body, which, as will presently be seen, satisfies only spiritual needs.

The *Adullamites* hold a Caucus from time to time to conspire against the College System. They wear blue spectacles and false beards, and say the most awful things to one another. There are two ways of dispersing these anarchs. One is to suggest that working hours might be lengthened. The other is to convert the provider of muffins and cigars to Conservative Liberalism. To mention belling the cat would be simply indecent.

No one can tell the difference between a *Liberal Conservative* Caucus and a *Conservative Liberal* one. There is nothing in the world more innocent than either. The most dare-devil action they ever take is to move for the appointment of a Syndicate 'to consider what means, if any, can be discovered to prevent the Public Washing of Linen, and to report, if they can see straight, to the Non-placets.' The result is the formation of an invertebrate body, which sits for two years, with growing discomfort, on the clothes-basket containing the linen. When the Syndicate is so stupefied that it has quite forgotten what it is sitting on, it issues three minority reports, of enormous bulk, on some different subject. The reports are referred by the Council to the Non-placets, and by the Non-placets to the wastepaper basket. This is called 'reforming the University from within.'

At election times each of these two Caucuses meets to select for nomination those members of its own party who are most likely to be mistaken by the Non-placets for members of the other party. The best results are achieved when the nominees get mixed up in such a way that the acutest of Non-placets cannot divine which ticket represents which party. The system secures that the balance of power shall be most happily maintained, and that all Young Men in a Hurry shall be excluded.

The *Young Men in a Hurry* have no regular Caucus. They meet, by two and threes, in desolate places, and gnash their teeth.

The *Non-placet* Caucus exists for the purpose of distributing Church patronage among those of its members who have adhered immovably to the principles of the party.

All Caucuses have the following rule. At Caucus meetings which are only attended by one member (owing to that member's having omitted to summon the others), the said member shall be deemed to constitute a quorum, and may vote the meeting full powers to go on the square without further ceremony.

IV   ON ACQUIRING INFLUENCE

Now that you know about the parties and the Caucuses, your first business will be to acquire influence. Political influence may be acquired in exactly the same way as the gout; indeed, the two ends ought to be pursued concurrently. The method is to sit tight and drink port wine. You will thus gain the reputation of being a good fellow; and not a few wild oats will be condoned in one who is sound at heart, if not at the lower extremities.

Or, perhaps, you may prefer to qualify as a *Good Business Man*.

He is one whose mind has not been warped and narrowed by merely intellectual interests, and who, at the same time, has not those odious pushing qualities which are unhappily required for making a figure in business anywhere else. He has had his finger on the pulse of the Great World—a distant and rather terrifying region, which it is very necessary to keep in touch with, though it must not be allowed on any account to touch you. Difficult as it seems, this relation is successfully maintained by sending young men to the Bar with Fellowships of £200 a year and no duties. Life at the Bar, in these conditions, is very pleasant; and only good business men are likely to return. All business men are good; and it is understood they let who will be clever, provided he be not clever at their expense.

V   THE PRINCIPLES OF GOVERNMENT, OF DISCIPLINE (INCLUDING RELIGION), AND OF SOUND LEARNING

These principles are all deducible from the fundamental maxim, that the first necessity for a body of men engaged in the pursuit of learning is freedom from the burden of practical cares. It is impossible to enjoy the contemplation of truth if one is vexed and distracted by the sense of responsibility. Hence the wisdom of our ancestors devised a form of academic polity in which this sense is, so far as human imperfection will allow, reduced to the lowest degree. By vesting the sovereign authority in the Non-placets (technically known as the 'Senate' on account of the high average of their age), our forefathers secured that the final decision should rest with a body which, being scattered in country parsonages, has no corporate feeling whatever, and, being necessarily ignorant of the decisive considerations in almost all the business submitted to it, cannot have the sense of any responsibility, except it be the highest, when the Church is in danger. In the smaller bodies, called 'Boards,' we have succeeded only in minimising the dangerous feeling, by the means of never allowing anyone to act without first consulting at least twenty other people who are accustomed to regard him with well-founded suspicion. Other democracies have reached this pitch of excellence; but the academic democracy is superior in having no organised parties. We thus avoid all the responsibilities of party leadership (there are leaders, but no one follows them), and the degradations of party compromise. It is clear, moreover, that twenty independent persons, each of whom has a different reason for not doing a certain thing, and no one of whom will compromise with any other, constitute a most effective check upon the rashness of individuals.

I forgot to mention that there is also a body called the 'Council', which consists of men who are firmly convinced that they are business-like. There is no doubt that some of them are Good Business Men.

The principle of Discipline (including Religion) is that *'there must be some rules.'* If you inquire the reason, you will find that the object of rules is to relieve the younger men of the burdensome feeling of moral or religious obligation. If their energies are to be left unimpaired for the pursuit of athletics, it is clearly necessary to protect them against the weakness of their own characters. They must never be troubled with having to think whether this or that ought to be done or not: it should be settled by rules. The most valuable rules are those which ordain attendance at lectures and at religious worship. If these were not enforced, young men would begin too early to take learning and religion seriously; and that is well known to be bad form. Plainly, the more rules

CAUGHT IN THE ACT—"WHAT IS YOUR NAME, AND COLLEGE, SIR?"

19 'Caught in the Act' – an undergraduate smoking in academical dress apprehended by the Proctor and his constables outside Macmillan and Bowes shop in Trinity Street. Cartoon 1909.

you can invent, the less need there will be to waste time over fruitless puzzling about right and wrong. The best sort of rules are those which prohibit important, but perfectly innocent, actions, such as smoking in College Courts, or walking to Madingley on Sunday without academical dress. The merit of such regulations is that, having nothing to do with right or wrong, they help to obscure these troublesome considerations in other cases, and to relieve the mind of all sense of obligation towards society.

The Roman sword would never have conquered the world if the grand fabric of Roman Law had not been elaborated to save the man behind the sword from having to think for himself. In the same way the British Empire is the outcome of College and School discipline and of the Church Catechism.

The Principle of Sound Learning is that the noise of vulgar fame should never trouble the cloistered calm of academic existence. Hence, learning is called sound when no one has ever heard of it; and 'sound scholar' is a term of praise applied to one another by learned men who have no reputation outside the University, and a rather queer one inside it. If you should write a book (you had better not), be sure that it is unreadable; otherwise you will be called 'brilliant' and forfeit all respect. University printing presses exist, and are subsidised by Government, for the purpose of producing books which no one can read; and they are true to their high calling. Books are the sources of material for lectures. They should be kept from the young; for to read books and remember what you read, well enough to reproduce it, is called 'cramming' and this is destructive of all true education. The best way to protect the young from books is, first, to make sure that they shall be so dry as to offer no temptation; and, second, to store them in such a way that no one can find them without several years' training. A lecturer is a sound scholar, who is chosen to teach on the ground that he was once able to learn. Eloquence is not permissible in a lecture; it is a privilege reserved by statute for the Public Orator.

VI THE POLITICAL MOTIVE

You will begin, I suppose, by thinking that people who disagree with you and oppress you must be dishonest. Cynicism is the besetting and venial fault of declining youth, and disillusionment its last illusion. It is quite a mistake to suppose that real dishonesty is all common. The number of rogues is about equal to the number of men who always act honestly; and it is very small. The great majority would sooner behave honestly than not. The reason why they do not give way to this natural preference of humanity is that they are afraid that others will not; and the others do not because they are afraid that *they* will not. Thus it comes about that, while behaviour which looks dishonest is fairly common, sincere dishonesty is about as rare as the courage to evoke good faith in your neighbours by shewing that you trust them.

No; the Political Motive in the academic breast is honest enough. It is *Fear*—genuine, perpetual, heart-felt, timorousness. We shall see presently that all the Political Arguments are addressed to this passion. Have you ever noticed how people say, 'I'm *afraid* I don't . . .' when they mean, 'I *think* I don't . . .'?

The proper objects of Fear, hereafter to be called *Bugbears*, are (in order of importance):

> Giving yourself away;
> Females;
> What Dr.—— will say;
> The Public Washing of Linen;
> Socialism, otherwise Atheism;
> The Great World;
>   etc. etc. etc.

With the disclosure of this central mystery of academic politics, the theoretical part of our treatise is complete. The practical principles, to which we now turn, can nearly all be deduced from the nature of the political passion and of its objects.

The PRACTICE OF POLITICS may be divided under three heads: *Argument; The Conduct of Business; Squaring.*

VII ARGUMENT

There is only one argument for doing something; the rest are arguments for doing nothing.

The argument for doing something is that it is the right thing to do. But then, of course, comes the difficulty of making sure that it is right. Females act by mere instinctive intuition; but men have the gift of reflection. As Hamlet, the typical man of action, says:

> 'What is a man,
> If his chief good and market of his time
> Be but to sleep and feed? a beast, no more.
> Sure, he that made us with such large discourse,
> Looking before and after, gave us not
> That capability and god-like reason
> To fust in us unused.'

Now the academic person is to Hamlet as Hamlet is to a female; or, to use his own quaint phrase, a 'beast'; his discourse is many times larger, and he looks before and after many times as far. Even a little knowledge of ethical theory will suffice to convince you that all important questions are so complicated, and the results of any course of action are so difficult to foresee, that certainty, or even probability, is seldom, if ever, attainable. It follows at once that the only justifiable attitude of mind is suspense of judgment; and this attitude, besides being peculiarly congenial to the academic temperament, has the advantage of being comparatively easy to attain. There remains the duty of persuading others to be equally judicious, and to refrain from plunging into reckless courses which might lead them Heaven knows whither. At this point the arguments for doing nothing come in; for it is a mere theorist's paradox that doing nothing has just as many consequences as doing something. It is obvious that inaction can have no consequences at all.

Since the stone-axe fell into disuse at the close of the neolithic age, two other arguments of universal application have been added to the rhetorical armoury by the ingenuity of mankind. They are closely akin; and, like the stone-axe, they are addressed to the Political Motive. They are called the *Wedge* and the *Dangerous Precedent*. Though they are very familiar, the principles, or rules of inaction, involved in them are seldom stated in full. They are as follows.

The *Principle of the Wedge* is that you should not act justly now for fear of raising expectations that you may act still more justly in the future—expectations which you are afraid you will not have the courage to satisfy. A little reflection will make it evident that the Wedge argument implies the admission that the persons who use it cannot prove that the action is not just. If they could, that would be the sole and sufficient reason for not doing it, and this argument would be superfluous.

The *Principle of the Dangerous Precedent* is that you should not now do an admittedly right action for fear you, or your equally timid successors, should not have the courage to do right in some future case, which, *ex hypothesi*, is essentially different, but superficially resembles the present one. Every public action, which is not customary, either is wrong, or, if it is right, is a dangerous precedent. It follows that nothing should ever be done for the first time.

It will be seen that both the Political Arguments are addressed to the Bugbear of *Giving yourself away*. Other special arguments can be framed in view of the other Bugbears. It will often be sufficient to argue that a change is a change—an irrefutable truth. If this consideration is not decisive, it may be reinforced by the Fair Trial Argument—'*Give the present system a Fair Trial*.' This is especially useful in withstanding changes in the schedule of an examination. In this connection the exact meaning of the phrase is, 'I don't intend to alter my lectures if I can help it; and, if you pass this proposal, you will have to alter yours.' This paraphrase explains what might otherwise be obscure: namely, the reason why a Fair Trial ought only to be given to systems which already exist, not to proposed alternatives.

Another argument is that '*the Time is not Ripe*.' The Principle of Unripe Time is that people should not do at the present moment what they think right at that moment, because the moment at which they think it right has not yet arrived. But the unripeness of the time will, in some cases, be found to lie in the Bugbear, 'What Dr.—— will say.' Time, by the way, is like the medlar: it has a trick of going rotten before it is ripe.

ॐ

VIII   THE CONDUCT OF BUSINESS

This naturally divides into two branches: (1) *Conservative Liberal Obstruction*, and (2) *Liberal Conservative Obstruction*.

The former is by much the more effective; and it should always be preferred to mere unreasonable opposition, because it will bring you the reputation of being more advanced than any so-called reformer.

The following are the main types of argument suitable for the *Conservative Liberal*.

'The present measure would block the way for a far more sweeping reform.' The reform in question ought always to be one which was favoured by a few extremists in 1881, and which is by this time quite impracticable, and not even desired by any one. This argument may safely be combined with the Wedge argument: 'If we grant this, it will be impossible to stop short.' It is a singular fact that all measures are always opposed on both of these grounds. The apparent discrepancy is happily reconciled when it comes to voting.

Another argument is that *'the machinery for effecting the proposed objects already exists.'* This should be urged in cases where the existing machinery has never worked, and is now so rusty that there is no chance of its being set in motion. When this is ascertained, it is safe to add that *'it is far better that all reform should come from within'*; and to throw in a reference to the *Principle of Washing Linen*. This principle is that it is better never to wash your linen if you cannot do it without anyone knowing that you are so cleanly.

The third accepted means of obstruction is the *Alternative Proposal*. This is a form of Red Herring. As soon as three or more alternatives are in the field, there is pretty sure to be a majority against any one of them, and nothing will be done.

The method of *Prevarication* is based upon a very characteristic trait of the academic mind, which comes out in the common remark, 'I was in favour of the proposal until I heard Mr.—'s arguments in support of it.' The principle is, that a few bad reasons for doing something neutralise all the good reasons for doing it. Since this is devoutly believed, it is often the best policy to argue weakly against the side you favour. If your personal enemies are present in force, throw in a little bear-baiting, and you are certain of success. You can vote in the minority, and no one will be the wiser.

Liberal Conservative Obstruction is less argumentative and leans to invective. It is particularly fond of the Last Ditch and the Wild Cat.

The *Last Ditch* is the Safe Side (see p. 95), considered as a place which you may safely threaten to die in. You are not likely to die there prematurely; for, to judge by the look of the inhabitants, the climate of the Safe Side conduces to longevity. If you did die, nobody would much mind; but the threat may frighten them for the moment.

'*Wild Cat*' is an epithet applicable to persons who bring forward a scheme unanimously agreed upon by experts after a two years' exhaustive consideration of thirty-five or more alternative proposals. In its wider use it applies to all ideas which were not familiar in 1881.

There is an oracle of Merlin which says, 'When the wild cat is belled, the mice will vote *Placet*.'

The Argument, '*that you remember exactly the same proposal being rejected in 1867,*' is a very strong one in itself; but its defect is that it appeals only to those who also remember the year 1867 with affectionate interest, and, moreover, are unaware that any change has occurred since then. There are such people, but they are lamentably few; and some even of them are no longer Young Men in a Hurry, and can be trusted to be on the Safe Side in any case. So this argument seldom carries its proper weight.

When other methods of obstruction fail, you should have recourse to *Wasting Time;* for, although it is recognised in academic circles that time in general is of no value, considerable importance is attached to tea-time, and by deferring this, you may exasperate any body of men to the point of voting against anything. The simplest method is *Boring.* Talk slowly and indistinctly, at a little distance from the point. No academic person is ever voted into the chair until he has reached an age at which he has forgotten the meaning of the word 'irrelevant'; and you will be allowed to go on, until everyone in the room will vote with you sooner than hear your voice another minute. Then you should move for adjournment. Motions for adjournment, made less than fifteen minutes before tea-time or at any subsequent moment, are always carried. While you are engaged in Boring it does not much matter what you talk about; but, if possible, you should discourse upon the proper way of doing something which you are notorious for doing badly yourself. Thus, if you are an inefficient lecturer, you should lay down the law on how to lecture; if you are a good business man, you should discuss the principles of finance; and so on.

If you have applied yourself in youth to the cultivation of the *Private Business habit of mind* at the Union and other debating societies, questions of procedure will furnish you with many resources for wasting time. You will eagerly debate whether it is allowable or not to amend an amendment; or whether it is consonant with the eternal laws for a body of men, who have all changed their minds, to rescind a resolution which they have just carried. You will rise, like a fish, to points of order, and call your intimate friends 'honourable' to their faces. You will make six words do duty for one; address a harmless individual as if he were a roomful of abnormally stupid reporters; and fill up the time till you can think of something to say by talking, instead of by holding your tongue.

An appeal should be made, wherever it is possible, to *College Feeling*. This, like other species of patriotism, consists in a sincere belief that the institution to which you belong is better than an institution to which other people belong. The corresponding belief ought to be encouraged in others by frequent confession of this article of faith in their presence. In this way a healthy spirit of rivalry will be promoted. It is this feeling which makes the College System so valuable; and differentiates, more than anything else, a College from a boarding-house; for in a boarding-house hatred is concentrated, not upon rival establishments, but upon the other members of the same establishment.

Should you have a taste for winter sports, you may amuse yourself with a little *Bear-baiting* or *Bull-fighting*. Bulls are easier to draw than bears; you need only get to know the right red rag for a given bull, and for many of them almost any rag will serve the turn. Bears are more sulky and have to be prodded; on the other hand they don't go blind, like bulls; and when they have bitten your head off, they will often come round and be quite nice. Irishmen can be bulls, but not bears; Scotsmen can be bears, but not bulls; an Englishman may be either.

Another sport which wastes unlimited time is *Comma-hunting*. Once start a comma and the whole pack will be off, full cry, especially if they have had a literary training. (Adullamites affect to despise commas, and even their respect for syntax is often not above suspicion.) But comma-hunting is so exciting as to be a little dangerous. When attention is entirely concentrated on punctuation, there is some fear that the conduct of business may suffer, and a proposal get through without being properly obstructed on its demerits. It is therefore wise, when a kill has been made, to move at once for adjournment.

ર્જ્જ

IX SQUARING

This most important branch of political activity is, of course, closely connected with *jobs*. These fall into two classes, My Jobs and Your Jobs. My Jobs are public-spirited proposals, which happen (much to my regret) to involve the advancement of a personal friend, or (still more to my regret) of myself. Your Jobs are insidious intrigues for the advancement of yourself and your friends, speciously disguised as public-spirited proposals. The term Job is more commonly applied to the second class. When you and I have, each of us, a Job on hand, we shall proceed to go on the Square.

Squaring can be carried on at lunch; but it is better that we should meet casually. The proper course to pursue is to take a walk, between 2 and 4 p.m., up and down the King's Parade, and more particularly that part of it which lies between the Colleges of Pembroke and Caius. When we have thus succeeded in meeting accidentally, it is etiquette to talk about indifferent matters for ten minutes and then part. After walking five paces in the opposite direction you should call me back, and begin with the words, 'Oh, by the way, if you should happen . . .' The nature of Your Job must then be vaguely indicated, without mentioning names; and it should be treated by both parties as a matter of very small importance. You should hint that I am a very influential person, and that the whole thing is a secret between us. Then we shall part as before, and I shall call you back and introduce the subject of My Job, in the same formula. By observing this procedure we shall emphasise the fact that there is *no connection whatever* between my supporting your Job and your supporting mine. This absence of connection is the essential feature of Squaring.

Remember this: *the men who get things done are the men who walk up and down the King's Parade, from 2 to 4, every day of their lives.* You can either join them, and become a powerful person; or you can join the great throng of those who spend all their time in preventing them from getting things done, and in the larger task of preventing one another from doing anything whatever. This is the Choice of Hercules, when Hercules takes to politics.

෨

X FAREWELL

O young academic politician, my heart is full of pity for you, because you will not believe a word that I have said. You will mistake sincerity for cynicism, and half the truth for exaggeration. You will think the other half of the truth, which I have not told, is the whole. You will take your own way, make yourself dreadfully disagreeable, tread on innumerable toes, butt your head against stone walls, neglect prejudice and fear, appeal to reason instead of appealing to bugbears. Your bread shall be bitterness, and your drink tears.

I have done what I could to warn you. When you become middle-aged—on your five-and-thirtieth birthday—glance through this book and judge between me and your present self.

If you decide that I was wrong, put the book in the fire, betake yourself to the King's Parade, and good-bye. I have done with you.

But if you find that I was right, remember that other world, within the microcosm, the silent, reasonable world, where the only action is thought, and thought is free from fear. If you go back to it now, keeping just enough bitterness to put a pleasant edge on your conversation and just enough worldly wisdom to save other people's toes, you will find yourself in the best of all company—the company of clean, humorous, intellect; and if you have a spark of imagination, and try very hard to remember what it was like to be young, there is no reason why your brains should ever get woolly, or anyone should wish you out of the way. Farewell!

EXPLICIT

Acknowledgements

I have received a great deal of help in writing my part of this book. Three studies deserve special mention for the light they shed on the history of Cambridge at the end of the nineteenth century: D. A. Winstanley, *Later Victorian Cambridge* (Cambridge, 1947), Sheldon Rothblatt, *The Revolution of the Dons: Cambridge and Society in Victorian England* (2nd edition, Cambridge, 1981), and Christopher N. L. Brooke, *A History of the University of Cambridge*, vol. IV: *1870–1990* (Cambridge, 1993). An invaluable work of reference is J. R. Tanner (ed.), *The Historical Register of the University of Cambridge* (Cambridge, 1917; reprinted 1984). Albert O. Hirschman, *The Rhetoric of Reaction* (Cambridge, Mass., 1991), which was drawn to my attention by John Cathie, has much of interest to say in general about the type of argument parodied by Cornford in *Microcosmographia Academica*.

The Council of Trinity College, Cambridge, kindly allowed me to quote from their Minutes, and to reproduce the portraits of F. M. Cornford (frontispiece), Henry Jackson (15) and Henry Montagu Butler (16). The Principal and Fellows of Newnham College gave permission for the reproduction of Augustus John's portrait of Miss Harrison (1), the Master and Fellows of Gonville and Caius College for the photograph of Professor Ridgeway (17), the Syndics of the University Library for the portrait of Henry Jenkinson by John Singer Sargent (18). The Syndics also gave permission for the reproduction of the following photographs from the collections in the Map Room: (2) the Chancellor's procession, 11 June 1892 (University X. 2. 44); (3) Gonville and Caius College and the Senate-House from the south, *c*. 1900 (Views bb. 53 (2) 90. 8/2; (4) honorary degrees, 1894 (Views bb. 53 (2) 89. 1); (5) Proclamation of King Edward VII (Views bb. 53 (2) 90. 1); (8) the declaration of the poll (Views bb. 53 (2) 89. 2); (12) visit of King Edward VII (University X. 2. 87); and (14) interior of the University Library, *c*. 1900 (Views bb. 53 (2) 89. 15). The photograph of the laying of the foundation stone of Selwyn College Chapel (6) is reproduced by courtesy of the Council of Selwyn College. The following pictures are from the Cambridgeshire Collection in the Cambridge City Library, Lion Yard, and are reproduced with the permission of Cambridgeshire Libraries: (7) the vote on the admission of women to the titles of degrees (S. 1897); (10) the entrance to the Cavendish Laboratory (D2 Cav. KO. 33457); (11) a laboratory in the Cavendish (D2 Cav. KO 15649); (13) the Botanical School, Downing Site, 1904 (D2 Bot. K04 15637); (19) 'Caught in the Act' (VW J87 19090) The plan of the development of the New Museums and Downing sites (9) is adapted from those in R.B. Pugh (ed.), *The Victoria History of the Counties of England. A History of the County of Cambridge and the Isle of Ely*, vol. III (London, 1959), p. 274.

The staff of the University Library have been unfailingly helpful, especially those in the Rare Books Room and the Map Room. Fred Ratcliffe, the Librarian allowed me to work conveniently on the *University Reporter* outside his office; Roy Welbourn made it simple for me to obtain xerox copies of difficult things; Roger Fairclough helped with the pictures; and David Hall eased the task of obtaining copies and the necessary permission for their reproduction. Anne Neary, the Archivist at Gonville and Caius College, suggested the photograph of Professor Ridgeway. Mrs Eyres at Selwyn College Library gave me easy access to the *Cambridge Review*, and Edward Ford kindly arranged for a new print to be made of the photograph from the Selwyn Archives. Trinity came to my rescue when it seemed that all the other copies in the University of Winstanley's *Later Victorian Cambridge* had disappeared into the hands of other readers. I am especially grateful to John Easterling, David McKitterick and the library staff at Trinity, who responded speedily and efficiently to a surprisingly large number of enquiries and requests. Mica Panić urged me to insert 1990 prices for some of the money values given in the book, and he kindly provided the relevant indices to enable me to do so. At the University Press, William Davies and Kevin Taylor both contributed significantly to the final form of the book. Linda Randall has been a superb copy-editor. Nicholas Cranfield prevented me from making two significant errors of fact, and he also very kindly read the proofs. Such anomalies and inconsistencies which remain in the text did not escape his eagle eye but stand as testimony to the vagaries of the English language and its printed usage.

A number of people read and commented on the penultimate version of my typescript. I am particularly grateful to Owen Chadwick, Anthony Edwards, Stephen Fleet, Faith Johnson, Geoffrey Lloyd and Robert Robson. I owe a special thanks, however, to Jeremy Mynott, who thought I 'might find it an amusing commission' to write a short new preface to a reissue of *Microcosmographia Academica*, and did not blench very much when it all got out of hand.

GORDON JOHNSON